How to draw like a
FASHION
ILLUSTRATOR

How to draw like a FASHION ILLUSTRATOR

Skills and techniques to develop your visual style

ARCTURUS

ARCTURUS

This edition published in 2015 by Arcturus Publishing Limited
26/27 Bickels Yard, 151–153 Bermondsey Street,
London SE1 3HA

ISBN: 978-1-78404-636-1
AD004580UK

Printed in China

CONTENTS

INTRODUCTION

This book looks at how to draw a fashion figure, developing techniques such as proportion, balance and other skills you will need to achieve striking results as an illustrator. It suggests exercises for loosening up and experimenting with your own style, and demonstrates how different garments react to and drape the body – literally, how they clothe the figure. After that you can try your hand at the more challenging issues such as drawing pattern, texture, stripes and plaids.

It is nearly 25 years since I first started exploring the idea of becoming a fashion illustrator. From an early age I had wanted to draw – it was the only thing that truly made me feel happy. I feel very fortunate that I've been able to make a living from doing something I love.

Getting started as an illustrator is a combination of hard work and good luck. On graduating, I was fortunate enough to be accepted at Victor Edelstein, an old-school couturier in Mayfair, London. The clientele was made up of very wealthy women who wanted clothing with flattering cuts in luxurious fabrics. It was a great chance to see a professional at work, designing for some very demanding clients. The attention to detail was phenomenal; I drew Victor's fashion designs either from mock-ups (known as toiles) or from his initial sketches. Several of my drawings were used in a brochure for his couture show in London. This was a great opportunity for my work to be seen by leading editors of British fashion magazines, and led to a call from *Vogue*.

This first commission started me on the path I'm still on – it hasn't always been steady, but it's certainly been enjoyable. It required determination and, more importantly, passion.

Inspiration

When I started out, inspiration was to be found in old leather-bound volumes of back copies of *Vogue*. I would spend hours poring over these in the library of my art college. They were full of drawings from the 40s and 50s, a golden period of illustration, and contained wonderful sketches by Marcel Vertés, Christian Bérard, René Gruau, Carl Erickson ('Eric') and René Bouet-Willaumez, among others. They were a remarkable resource for anyone interested in illustration.

The drawings dated from a time when photography wasn't allowed in magazines or at the big couture houses, so the new collections were captured by illustrators. This way of documenting fashion has seen a resurgence in recent years, as the Internet has opened up a world of resources, from museum websites and stock image sites to multifaceted sources of inspiration, such as Pinterest.

By looking back at successful illustrators from different eras, you often hit upon a long-forgotten style that has a resonance in the modern world and can be given a fresh lease of life by way of an unconventional perspective. This has frequently worked for me. When I start a drawing, the hardest part is the first mark on the blank piece

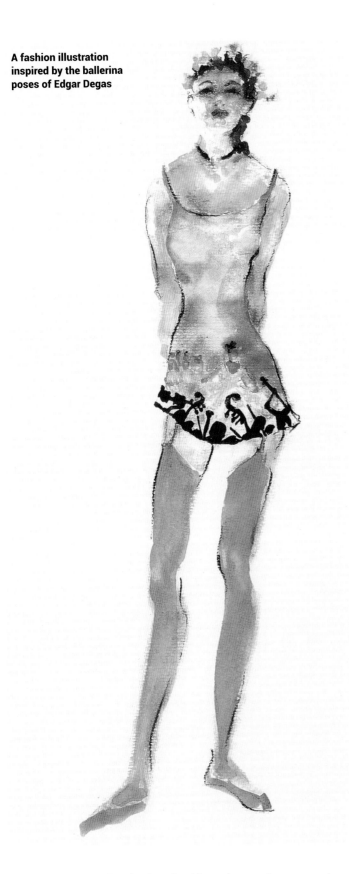

A fashion illustration inspired by the ballerina poses of Edgar Degas

regard to recording the hands in a realistic manner, but is more concerned with capturing the spirit of movement and the essence of the moment, and her work is all the more exhilarating for it.

Fine artists such as Toulouse-Lautrec, Matisse or Degas can inspire and enlighten your work with their wonderful use of line and colour. Toulouse-Lautrec shows how to capture the character of an individual with an astonishing economy of line; the dynamic quality of his brushstrokes tells you that the painting has been done at pace, but with a skill that comes only from confidence. Gaining that confidence takes practice. Toulouse-Lautrec spent his nights endlessly drawing the characters who inhabited the bars and clubs of Paris. Similarly, Matisse's figures possess a colour and boldness that is intoxicating, and using his paper cut-outs as templates is a great way to get started with collage.

I draw quickly; I hate having to sit and draw the same thing for more than half an hour. In life-drawing classes, I move around sketching the model from different angles otherwise I get bored and it shows in the drawing. While, unlike Toulouse-Lautrec, we no longer have access to the bars and bordellos of 19th-century Paris, sketching backstage at a fashion show has a similar sense of chaotic movement and fleeting moments. Just being in among the anarchy and glamour and trying to capture a beautiful model in an outfit or, better still, managing to nail the spirit of the whole show is exhilarating.

Vivienne Westwood's designs, with her wonderful silhouettes, historical references and use of fabrics, encapsulate the movement and passion that swirls around at a fashion show. Trying to capture tartan in an easy and uncontrived way is hard enough, but doing so surrounded by the distractions and noise of a party atmosphere and the great characters and stridently individual models who Westwood uses is enough to test the hardiest of souls.

Getting your personality across

Expressing yourself artistically is a very individual process and you should experiment widely and always be open to surprises. The objective is not to set yourself rules or habits for their own sake, but to find the tools you need to say what you want to say. Confidence plays a big part in this; some people are happy to use a chunky marker pen from the off, others may be worried about making a

of paper. If I need to be inspired by other artists to make this mark, then I am happy to do so. Most illustrators have had to learn their style and technique from someone with experience – only a very few are genuinely unique. Take Gladys Perint Palmer, for example, whose work has the freedom and looseness of Toulouse-Lautrec. She pays no

mistake; they may prefer to use an HB pencil or something else that can easily be erased.

A successful illustrator of children's books once told me that when she started out she was influenced by early Russian animators. She had some success in getting her books published, but then the work seemed to dry up. So she went and did some more research and tried drawing in an American 50s style, but, again, after some initial interest, the work didn't really take off. Throughout this period she continued going out and sketching things that interested her in a hardback sketchbook. It was while looking through some of these books of her drawings, with their strong, bold lines, that a question struck her: 'Why use other people's styles when there is a perfectly acceptable natural style all of my own, staring me in the face?' Once she started to work in her own unique way, the commissions began to flood in.

Learning from the past

Without a working knowledge of the artists and illustrators of the past, it is impossible to create for the future. Pioneers such as Georges Lepape and Paul Iribe illustrated the gorgeous garments of Paul Poiret, a couturier who inspired modern designers such as John Galliano and Alexander McQueen. Although the poses may look wooden by modern standards, their compositions and background details reward study. The figures have a doll-like quality, with delicately rounded hands that are no longer seen in contemporary drawings.

Artists who have inspired me include Egon Schiele, whose ground-breaking approach to figurative painting is still relevant today. I've often happened upon one of his drawings by accident and thought, 'Wow, what a great piece of contemporary illustration!', only to realize that it's a Schiele sketch, probably drawn over a hundred years ago. Léon Bakst produced wonderfully theatrical costume illustrations, heady with oriental details

and full of pattern, colour and the flowing grace of dance. He's a great artist to look at for ideas regarding layout and pose. His works for the Ballets Russes are superb. Bakst's brilliant control of colour, line and decoration give his stage illustrations a visual flow in which colour is used emotionally and sensuously. Look at his work alongside that of Erté (Romain de Tirtoff), a Russian-born French artist and designer who created over-the-top, stylized images of women in theatrical settings, overflowing with exaggerated poses and costumes.

Christian Bérard, another artist who also worked in theatre design, produced elegantly feminine, fluid work. He was heavily

A quick sketch of models waiting backstage at a Vivienne Westwood show in Paris

Mother and Child, a crayon drawing by Egon Schiele from 1918

for the work of some of today's foremost practitioners. They include Michael Roberts, Zak, Ruben Toledo, Gladys Perint Palmer, Jean-Phillippe Delhomme, Francois Berthoud, Mats Gustafson, Tanya Ling and Julie Verhoeven.

Helping you find your own style, something as unique and personal to you as the hands you draw with, is the ultimate goal of this book, and there is no one, single way of achieving this. Although the artists I have mentioned may have been influenced by similar aesthetics, they have each taken different paths in their work. Considering each illustrator as part of a continuum can help us all find our own place in the process.

influenced by Roman art, which shows that even the greatest illustrators took their inspiration from others. Carl Erickson – known simply as Eric – dominated the field of fashion illustration for over 35 years, spanning the 20s, 30s, 40s and 50s. He is often associated with another giant of fashion illustration, René Bouet-Willaumez, who refined his style through a daring use of colour as an element of his brisk, clear designs. His illustrations had a dramatic sense of style and command of space that masterfully sums up the period.

Antonio Lopez's work captured the mood of the 70s. His portrayal of modern women breaking boundaries was revolutionary as well as visually breathtaking. He worked with stars such as Grace Jones, Jessica Lange and Jerry Hall to create extraordinary poses. No list of illustrators would be complete without mentioning Zoltan, an original fashion illustrator who combined his drawings with fabrics, flowers, gems and other organic and inorganic materials to create striking textures and shapes.

To understand the rich diversity of contemporary illustration, keep a look out

A fashion portrait by Eric

Chapter 1

WHERE DO I START?

The tools and materials you use for your drawings will help to convey your individual style. If you can't decide what to use at first, then experiment. You will soon find the medium you feel most comfortable with.

DIFFERENT MEDIA

Watercolour

Watercolour is great for loose, sweeping strokes, but also good for fine detail. It's available in pans or tubes, and which you use is a matter of personal preference. Make sure you buy professional, or artist, quality colours: at college, I was one for a bargain so I used student quality, which look great while you are using them, but lose their vibrancy once they have dried.

With watercolour, you use flat brushes to cover large areas with a 'wash' and round brushes that taper to a fine point for figure work (nos. 8–12 are best). All brushes come in synthetic or natural hair, with sable the most expensive. Sable are great to use, but they don't make your work any better, just a tiny bit easier. Synthetic brushes are good too – try a few in different sizes and you'll soon work out which are best for you.

Before starting to paint, make sure you've a couple of jars of clean water handy – one for rinsing brushes, the other to use generally (otherwise you'll soon have a jar of muddy water which will ruin your picture). It's good to have some toilet paper handy to mop up wet areas or mistakes.

Watercolour has a great transparent quality. For precise detail, sharp edges and no colour running, apply colour with a nearly dry brush, using just enough water to grab the colour (dry brush technique). For soft-edged marks and natural-looking transitions of different colours, use a damp brush to apply colour to damp paper (wet on wet technique). For greater control and more defined edges, use a moist brush on dry paper (wet on dry technique).

Coloured pencils

I don't use these very often, but they are great for detailed drawing that requires lots of control, and techniques such as layering, with cross-hatching, blending and other different strokes. An eraser is useful in this instance. The choice of paper type is up to you – smooth paper is great for creating glossy images; textured paper catches the colours more readily. Watersoluble pencils enable you to blend your mark-making with water for a more painterly effect.

Inks

For strong, vibrant colour, try inks. These can look incredible when blended on really wet paper – the bleeds create their own interest. You need to exercise control so that the medium does not overpower the design. Black ink with a dipping pen is something I use a lot, especially when I want crisp, thin lines to show delicacy and detail. There is still an element of chance as ink is likely to splatter occasionally, especially if you are using quick, hard lines which are great for edgy drawing.

Charcoal

I highly recommend using charcoal sticks for life drawings. They are great for creating bold, heavy marks and smudgy shaded areas. If you think you've made a mistake, just smudge over it with your hand and redraw. I love it when I press too hard and the stick crackles and snaps! Charcoal pencils are also great for detailed linework. They range from soft to hard, with the harder ones best for more detailed work.

Collage

This is a great way to start with illustration, especially if you want strong colour added quickly and boldly. If you want to create, say, a gingham print, an effective way of doing it is to cut strips of tissue paper and glue them horizontally and then vertically to express the bold characteristics of the fabric.

Marker pens

I've recently started using marker pens and I love them, as the range of colours is terrific and they are a strong way of expressing line. But, be warned, they're not for the faint-hearted! Maybe start by using some of the softer pastel shades and build up your confidence. I love the chiselled tip, which allows you to create two different thickness of line; the double-ended ones are also great. For finer work, use fine-liner, felt-tip nib pens. Have fun and experiment!

Pastels

The advantage of pastels is that you don't have to wait for the colours to dry; they are great to blend or draw over to create unblended strokes.

When blending colours, you do it directly on the paper instead of with, for example, gouache, where you use a mixing palette. The paper needs to have a texture for the pastel to stick. Ingres, watercolour or rough rice paper are all good, and your results will be even better if you use a coloured paper. I've used black paper in the example. If you store your pastels in one big box, they will rub against one another and get dirty. Trying placing them in a box of sawdust or uncooked rice and shaking it – they will come out as good as new.

Gouache

Gouache is more opaque than watercolour. It dries quickly so you can paint layers on top. You can dilute it with water for washes or use it straight from the tube and apply with brushes, sponges or palette knives – anything that might give an interesting texture. In the example above I've used gouache in soft washes and then applied it more thickly for the detailing over the background colour.

LIFE DRAWING AND LINE

Drawing from life, with a clothed or naked subject in a studio, or just drawing people you see in the street, is a great way to hone your skills at rendering a good and convincing figure. Knowing how the body connects together in different poses will increase your confidence and lead you to better results.

Life drawing is the basis of all art and a practice you should never give up, no matter how long you've been drawing. If you aren't lucky enough to attend classes, either through college or run by your local council or privately, you can draw your friends clothed. When you first begin, it is best to have models in garments that don't obscure or distort the body too much. You need to be reasonably practised before you start changing the silhouette and experimenting with the body's shape.

Backgrounds

The way in which a body fits into a scene is really important – for example, the scale of a building outside which a couple are eating, and that of the table, food, chairs and waiter in relation to the central figures. Drawing scenes with backgrounds will help you gain a sense of proportion.

A great way to draw clothed figures is on public transport – on a train or waiting for a bus. Most journeys last at least 15 minutes, which is plenty of time to capture the likeness of a person sitting in a relaxed manner. Look at the draping and the shape of the clothing and add some personality to the facial features. Don't just use young people as your models, but a wide range of

characters. You'll soon get an idea of the kind of figures you prefer to draw and this will show in your work. Any size of pad can be used, just something you feel comfortable carrying around with you and whipping out when a subject appears. But remember, not everyone wants to be captured on paper, so be sensitive to this!

Don't bother using expensive paper or materials for these sketches – plain newsprint paper is great or even old newspapers (especially if you find it daunting to make the first marks on a pristine sheet of white paper). Brown wrapping paper, lining paper, wallpaper, striped sweet bags and old envelopes are all great surfaces. I sometimes make a collage, using newsprint for the darker shaded areas and the figures, ripping it and sticking it down with a glue stick, then drawing on top with charcoal.

Line

Line is very subjective, a bit like writing your signature. It should give you a sense of the garment – the form, cut, textile. This is where the focus should be, not on the figure; the star should be the outfit. Therefore don't pay too much attention to the linework on the unclothed parts of the figure when you are starting out.

When using a brush to create your linework, think about the type of lines you want to use for different fabrics – fast and scratchy or slow and smooth, short and controlled – and work out which are best for capturing the feel of your subject.

Think about the different fabrics. A fuzzy, blurred line applied with the dry brush technique works well for wool and mohair. A quick, crisp line is best for taffeta. Silk should have a sensuous, undulating line. Chiffon calls for soft, short, straight lines. Look at a range of fabrics and see how they move differently; hold them up and let them drape, move them around to see what kind of folds they create. Are they smooth, big, even folds or crisp and too numerous to count? Where does the light fall on the folds? How will the fabric react to being folded around a body? Silk will hug a figure and move with it and taffeta will stick out at crazy angles. Think how you might want to represent these different characteristics.

Scale

Find out what size of paper is best for you – maybe drawing in a pocket-sized sketch book or life size, using rolls of lining paper. When I first started painting fashion figures, I used 3m (10 ft) sheets of cardboard nailed to the wall and drew Amazonian women with charcoal and ink, revelling in the inky dribbles that ran down the sheets! But this might not be right for you, so experiment and find out what suits you best.

WARM-UP EXERCISES

Keep a sketchbook with you at all times; the spontaneity of a doodle can capture your natural style. Treat this as something that is yours alone – if nobody else looks through your book, you will not feel judged (which can be inhibiting).

Look through your tear sheets (your favourite pages ripped out of fashion magazines) for some faces that interest you and draw a series of stylized versions based on specific looks, for example, a high-end runway look, a beach blonde surfer chick, or a fashion-forward teen. Use the hairstyle, makeup, attitude and accessories to help push this look to the extreme.

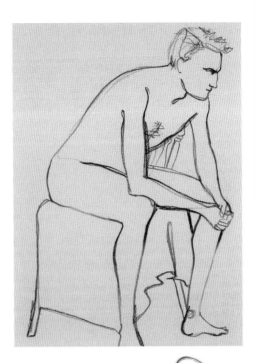

Exercise 1

To get warmed up, take a pen or marker and a clean piece of paper and fill it with the figure 8. Make a continuous line drawing, just looking at the figure and not the paper. The more you practise this, the better you'll get! Now draw the rough outline of a friend or life model seated or standing.

Exercise 2

Draw a friend or life model dressed in big, bold patterns. Start your drawing with the feet and work your way up the figure (most people instinctively work from the head down). If you are using colour, block in the main colours of the garments then get to grips with the pattern. Block in the head, feet and arms in a skin tone. Don't draw any outlines – instead, use the contrasting patterns and colours to define the figure.

Exercise 3

Now draw the space around the figure – the negative spaces between the limbs. Block in the spaces between the arms and torso, and the space between the legs.

Exercise 4

This exercise is a bit 'left field', but worth a try! Instead of paper and pen, use wire to make your drawing. Try not to fight the medium, but work with its properties. You will not be able to 'draw' tight corners, but you should be able to manage a flowing continuous line. The unwieldy quality of the wire means that you will concentrate on the essence of the figure rather than on small details.

Chapter 2 BODY BASICS

This chapter explains how to draw the proportions of your figure. Once you've got the basics sorted you can exaggerate the body as you see fit. Your personal style will be established through experimentation and finding what's right for you – although there is a theory that illustrators all draw their alter egos!

FEMALE FIGURE TEMPLATE

STEP 1

Using a sheet of A5, A4 or A3, depending on whatever size of paper you feel comfortable working with, draw a vertical line (called the balance line) all the way down the sheet. I usually work with A3, and start with a 4cm (1.5in) head height, which makes it easier when working out quarters. Start near the top of sheet to give yourself plenty of room to draw the whole figure. Measure down the balance line in 4cm (1.5in) sections. You will have nine in total, including the head. If you are working on A3 paper, you can increase this to 5cm (2in) sections, if you prefer.

STEP 2

Draw an oval for the head in the first section and then follow the measurements in the diagram, which shows the shoulders, waist, hips and knees with the appropriate measurements blocked in. A head length of 4cm (1.5in) = 1 section.

STEP 3

Now work out the widths of the proportions: shoulders are 1.5 head lengths wide; waist is 0.75 of a head length wide; low hip is 1.25 head lengths wide.

STEP 4

Work out the arm length: the upper arm should be just a bit longer than the shoulder-to-waist measurement; the forearm should end just past the widest part of the hip; and the hand should be roughly three-quarters of the head height.

STEP 5

You've now drawn the basic body proportion. It may be quite messy, with lots of erasures and redrawn lines, so put a new piece of paper or tracing paper over the top and trace over it. First draw the balance line so that you can keep everything in place and to ensure your drawing is symmetrical. You can adjust areas until you have a figure guide you feel comfortable with.

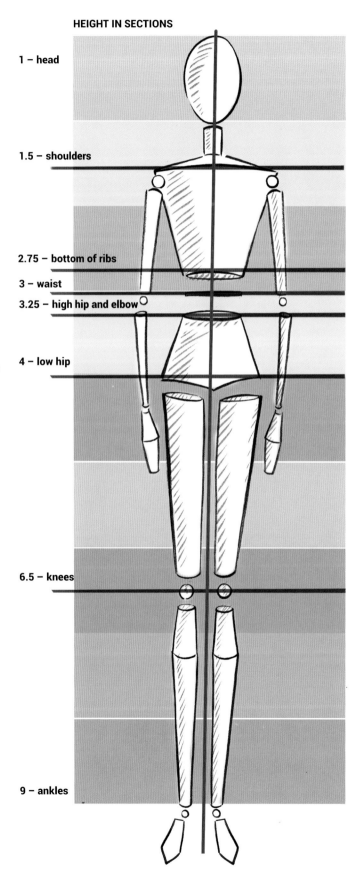

HEIGHT IN SECTIONS

1 – head

1.5 – shoulders

2.75 – bottom of ribs

3 – waist

3.25 – high hip and elbow

4 – low hip

6.5 – knees

9 – ankles

FASHION FIGURE TEMPLATE

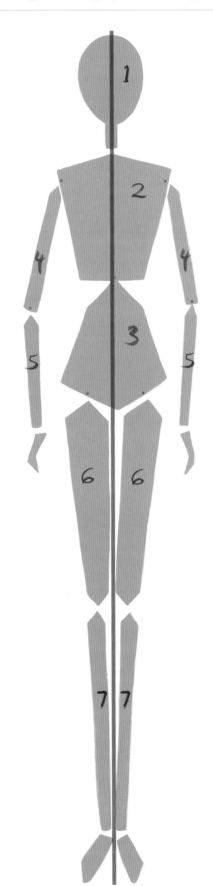

This template will help you draw a figure to fashion proportions. If you prefer, you can draw your figure on darker paper so you can see it clearly. Number the various body parts before cutting them out.

STEP 1

Following the steps on page 17, draw the balance line all the way down the sheet of paper. Start near the top of the sheet to give yourself plenty of space to draw the whole figure. Measure down the balance line in 4cm (1.5in) sections, making nine in total.

STEP 2

Draw an oval for the head in the first section, then follow this with the torso and legs.

STEP 3

Now draw the arms and hands.

STEP 4

Label the parts as shown, to avoid confusion once you've cut them out.

You Will Need
- ★ smooth paper
- ★ HB or B pencil
- ★ ruler
- ★ black fine-tip marker pen
- ★ tape
- ★ tracing paper

Adjusting your pose

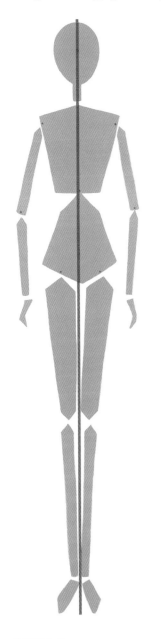

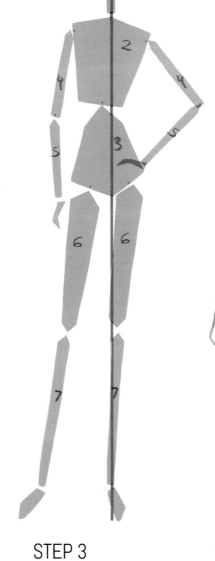
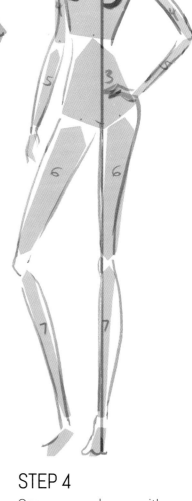

STEP 1

On a clean piece of paper, draw in the balance line. Arrange your cut figure pieces in the original pose, using the balance line as a guide.

STEP 2

Move the hip area slightly to create a high-hip pose and adjust the torso/ shoulder to allow for this (it should be opposite to the hip angle). Make sure the body parts are still connected in the right areas, and stick them down with tape (use masking tape if you are planning to readjust them to different positions).

STEP 3

Experiment with the leg placement to get a feel of what looks right and what seems unbalanced. Look at your tear sheets for simple standing front-view poses (no walking or three-quarter turned figures), and try to replicate them.

STEP 4

Once you are happy with your version, put a sheet of tracing paper over the top and trace the various elements. Draw in a more realistic figure using the template as your guide.

PROPORTION

Use the basic template on the previous page to help with the consistency of the proportions and to create a fluid image. Drawing from life will give you a sense of the body's structure and enable you to progress more quickly.

Stylized proportion can be anything you want, as long as it works well with the designs and is consistent across your range of drawings. My early drawings had incredibly long torsos, with breasts halfway down! At the most charitable, these might be described as 'charming in a naive way'.

Try experimenting with a range of, say, four figures in different proportions: tall, toned Amazonian; demure, elfin; waif; and big-headed alien. You'll soon get a feel for which pleases you most and you'll find yourself enjoying spending more time on those. Alternatively, take a look at your existing drawings and work out how many heads they contain. If they vary wildly, work out which feels better to you and use that ratio – it'll feel more natural and will allow you to work towards developing your own sense of proportion. At this stage, don't waste too much time on the hands, toes and facial features; we shall talk about those later in the book.

Skeleton to fashion sketch

Modern fashion tends towards very slender models. I'm really not happy if you can see individual ribs and hip-bones jutting out – it looks extremely unhealthy and may be seen to glamorize anorexia. Your illustrations should portray a slender figure so that the clothes take centre stage, not the body inside them. It may be a fantasy figure, but it helps to have some semblance of reality, and a nod to the underlying bone structure will help to give your drawing conviction. Just don't get too carried away with lumps and bumps – the female fashion drawing should have a soft, fluid line to it.

Here are some poses achieved from the previous spine positions. Make your own sketches of small 'stick figures' to experiment with the angles of the body parts and how they react with one another. See how the shoulder angle works in opposition to the hip angle and the spine curves away from the side of the dropped shoulder and high hip.

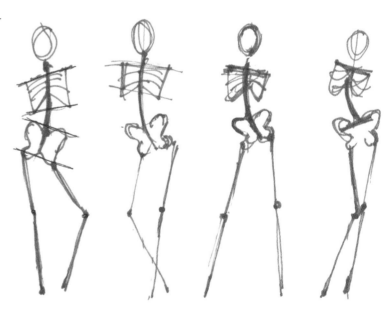

Look at the skeleton and see how the different sections operate individually and together. In the first diagram you can see that the right shoulder is high, which means that the right hip will be low (shoulder and hip angles act in opposition). This side of the torso is stretched and the left side is contracted. The shoulder, spine and hip always work in this relationship – it is a very important fundamental rule which helps when you are constructing poses. Draw a few of each of these diagrams.

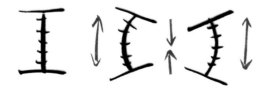

Three different spine positions.

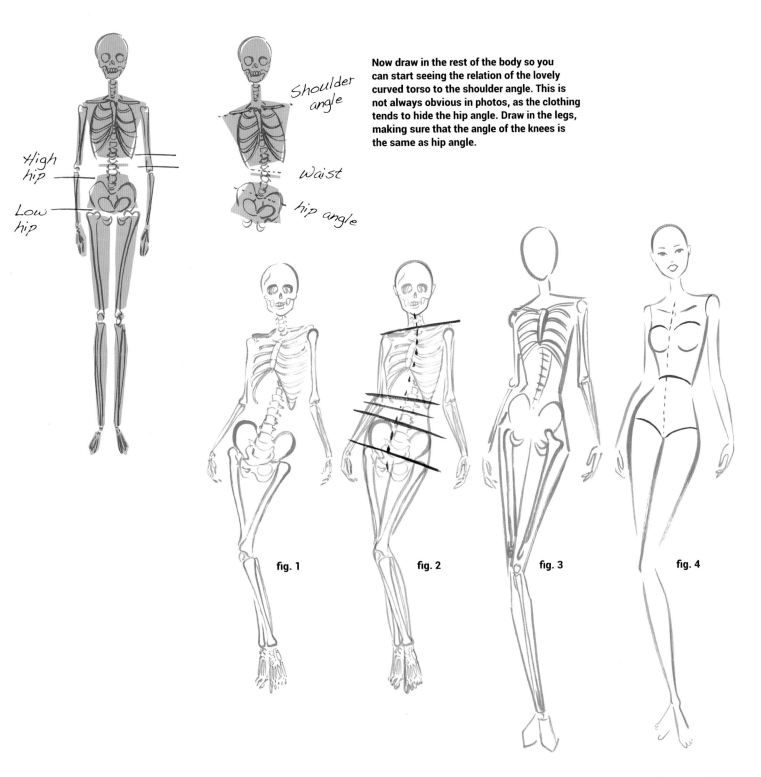

High hip

Low hip

Shoulder angle

Waist

hip angle

Now draw in the rest of the body so you can start seeing the relation of the lovely curved torso to the shoulder angle. This is not always obvious in photos, as the clothing tends to hide the hip angle. Draw in the legs, making sure that the angle of the knees is the same as hip angle.

fig. 1   fig. 2   fig. 3   fig. 4

fig. 1: This is what the skeleton does when the body is in high-hip pose. The bottom of the ribcage and the top of the left hip become closer and the right side is stretched, creating a lovely curve.

fig. 2: Here the body's shape is seen with the skeletal structure underneath. See how the red lines showing the angles follow the bone structure. The dotted line shows the sweep of the spine.

fig. 3: This shows the unnatural fashion illustration proportions. The natural bone structure is changed to accommodate this and the ribs and hips are narrower. Notice how the knee is higher up on the side with the higher hip. I've marked the areas where the bone may be more visible near the surface.

fig. 4: This is the fashion template's scaled-up version of the natural figure. You can scale up this yourself using the template rules. Also marked is the centre front, which you will need for reference when you come to clothe your figure. Now place a clean piece of tracing paper over the rough template you've just made and draw a fashion proportioned body, adding the centre front, waist angle, bust-lines and armholes – these are all useful reference points when creating your garment sketch.

PROPORTION – BODY BLOCKING

This is a fun, loose, experimental way of finding your preferred fashion illustration proportion. It's great for people like me, who don't want to get bogged down with too much science and maths when creating something which should feel free and natural. It's quite different from the more rigid cut-out technique.

Regardless of how tall the model is, the widest part of the hip is halfway down the body, where I've made a red mark. It's worth remembering that the head and torso comprise one half of a person's total height. But as this is a fashion drawing, the proportions are distorted for effect and the legs are made extra long. The equivalent of two head lengths are added to the leg length.

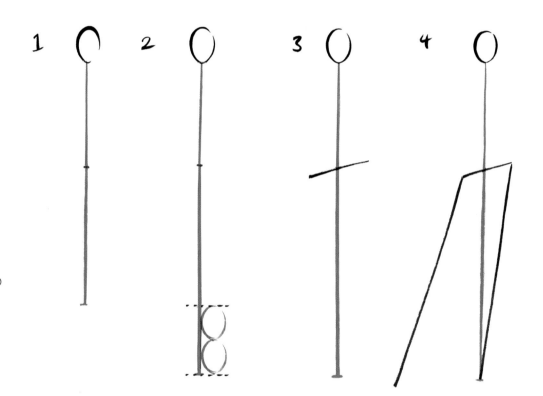

STEP 1

Draw in the oval head. I suggest doing this in pencil for the first few times. Next draw the balance line down to the roughly guessed height of your figure. Roughly mark in the centre point on the line; just use your eye, don't bother measuring.

STEP 2

Now add extra height at the bottom of the figure. This should be roughly twice the head length. You can do this by eye or by measuring with your fingers or a pencil.

STEP 3

Draw in the hip line at an angle at the marked halfway point. This length can be roughly guessed, but as a rule hip width is 1.75 heads.

STEP 4

Now draw in the supporting leg, as shown. It needs to hit the balance line at the bottom, so that the figure looks stable. Remember, just do easy poses as at this stage you are only interested in the proportions. Add the other leg after this.

STEP 5

Draw in the shoulders (these should be roughly 1.5 head lengths wide) and the waistline (0.75 of a head length wide). The shoulder line should be in opposition to the hip line. The waist follows the hip angle.

STEP 6

Draw in a curved dotted line, sweeping up at the waist. This shows you the elbow position. The knee joints follow the same angle as the hips, and are about halfway between hip and foot.

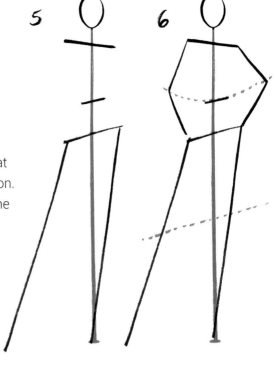

STEP 7

Now sketch in the torso to the hip. You can modify the bust size, making it larger or smaller – your choice, it's up to the feel of the figure.

STEP 8

Add the rest of the illustration, as shown. You've now drawn your first 'blocking method' figure. Using the same technique, draw a short and a tall figure to get an idea of the proportion you'd prefer to use in your drawings.

Here the figure is drawn on top of the body blocking template.

See how the balance line has been shortened and the halfway point marked. Two head lengths have been added to the bottom. You can see that the proportions still work if you follow the guide.

Here the balance line has been lengthened. The halfway point is marked and two head lengths are added to the bottom.

FRONT, BACK AND PROFILE

If you plan to use your illustrations in a garment portfolio, you will need to show front and back views. This is especially important when there are special features, such as low backs and asymmetric seams and openings. Profile views are also useful for showing line and drape.

The back view is best shown as a flipped version of the front, as here. Pay attention to the positioning of the arms, elbows and backs of knees and make sure they relate to the front view you've drawn. If, as in this image, the hand is placed on the waist showing the back of the hand and the knuckles, then the back view should show part of the palm and fingers. In the front view, the left knee is further forwards so this leg will be blocked slightly behind the other leg in the back view.

Remember to maintain the angle of the head in the back view. If you draw the head in profile for this, it can lead to confusion as to whether it's a front or a back view.

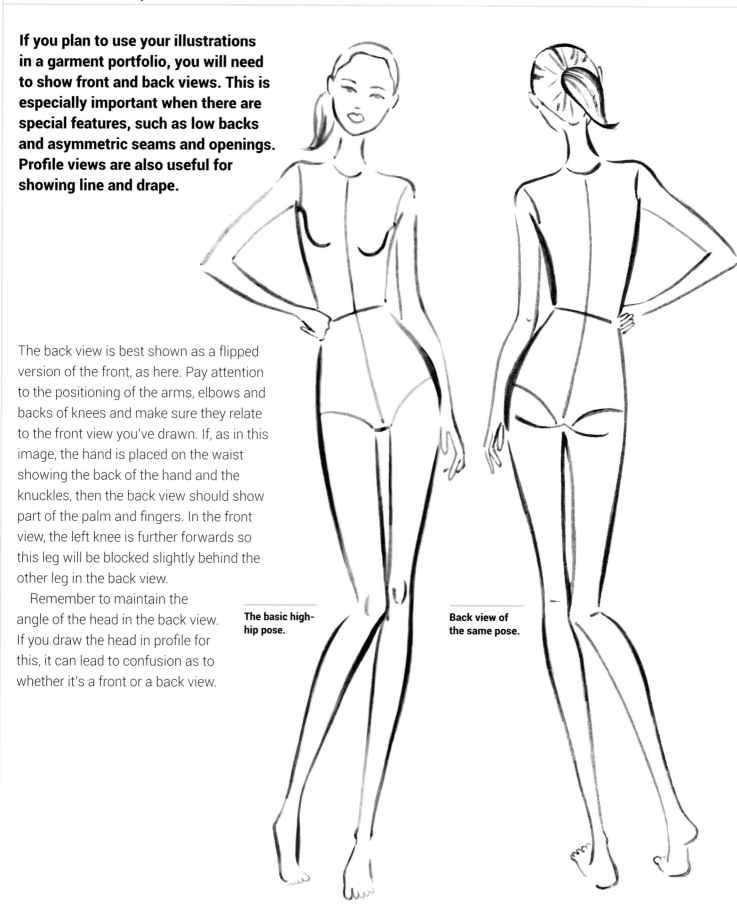

The basic high-hip pose.

Back view of the same pose.

Drawing the female figure in profile

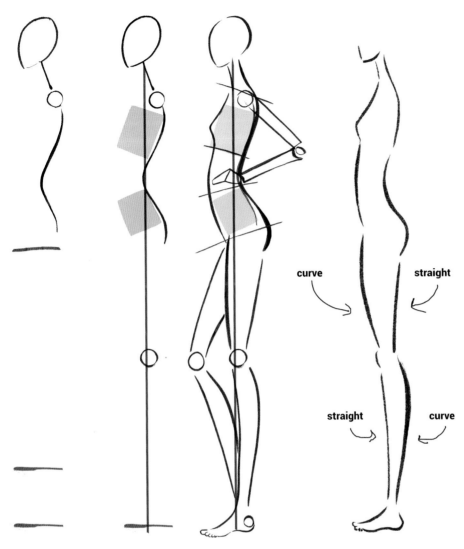

curve

straight

straight

curve

Notice how the weight is distributed around the balance line, which runs from the neck to the ball of the foot.

STEP 1
Here's how to do a quick profile. Draw a slightly tilted egg shape for the head at the top of the page. Use the technique on pages 22–3 to get the height of your character. Roughly mark in pencil where the legs and feet will finish. Draw in the neck, remembering that the angle tilts forwards, then draw a circle for the shoulder/arm joint and and an 'S' shape for the spine.

STEP 2
Drop a balance line down from where the top of the spine joins the head. Draw in a box shape for the ribcage and another for the hips, remembering that they will follow the angle of the spine. At the leg halfway point,

add a circle to the right side of the balance line for the knee. Don't make it too small.

STEP 3
Draw the outline of the body using the box shapes to guide you. Don't make the waist too small or there will be no room for design detail on your garment. Draw the back of the thigh as a straight line to the back of knee, and the front thigh muscle as a gentle curve.

STEP 4
Reverse this for the lower part of the leg, drawing the curve on the back of the leg for the calf muscle, with a straight line on the front of the leg for the shin.

Chapter 3 POSES

Knowing how to draw a convincing pose is the essence of fashion illustration. Once you've mastered this, you can start to have fun inventing more complicated and distorted poses to enhance your garment designs.

STRAIGHT-ON POSES

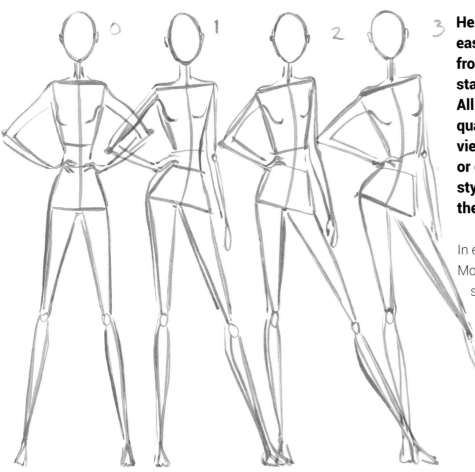

Here is a range of poses you can create easily by simply shifting the weight from one leg to the other. Use them as starting points for your illustrations. All are straight on – there are no three-quarter or contorted angles or side views. The hands are either by the side or on the hip. As you develop your own style, think what you can add to vary these poses.

In each case, the body has a centre front. Most clothing has an obvious centre front, shown via a v-neck on a sweater or buttons on shirts and cardigans, or buttons/zips on coats. It runs from the neckline down to the hemline of the garment. Even if it is not shown, the centre line is useful for placing zips, pockets, buttons and design details to make them symmetrical.

All these poses can be used as starting points for your own fashion poses. Experiment with different arm and head positions.

HIGH-HIP POSE

Here's a classic fashion pose called the 'high hip'. This is when the weight of the body rests entirely on one leg. It is a good way of starting to practise and experiment with further poses.

There are certain rules attached to this pose which will help to make your figures look natural and unforced. We won't complicate things by thinking about garments at this stage.

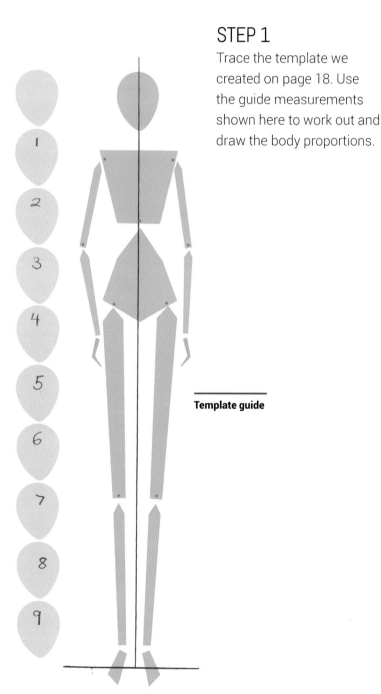

STEP 1

Trace the template we created on page 18. Use the guide measurements shown here to work out and draw the body proportions.

Template guide

STEP 2

For the high-hip pose, draw in the balance line. This should intersect the base of the neck and go straight down to where the foot taking all the weight is placed (in this case, on the left-hand side, as you look at it). This is the starting point for all your poses in this exercise, the aim of which is to show the range of poses you can achieve with the arms and the right leg. Copy this pose with your tracing paper or using the guide measurements.

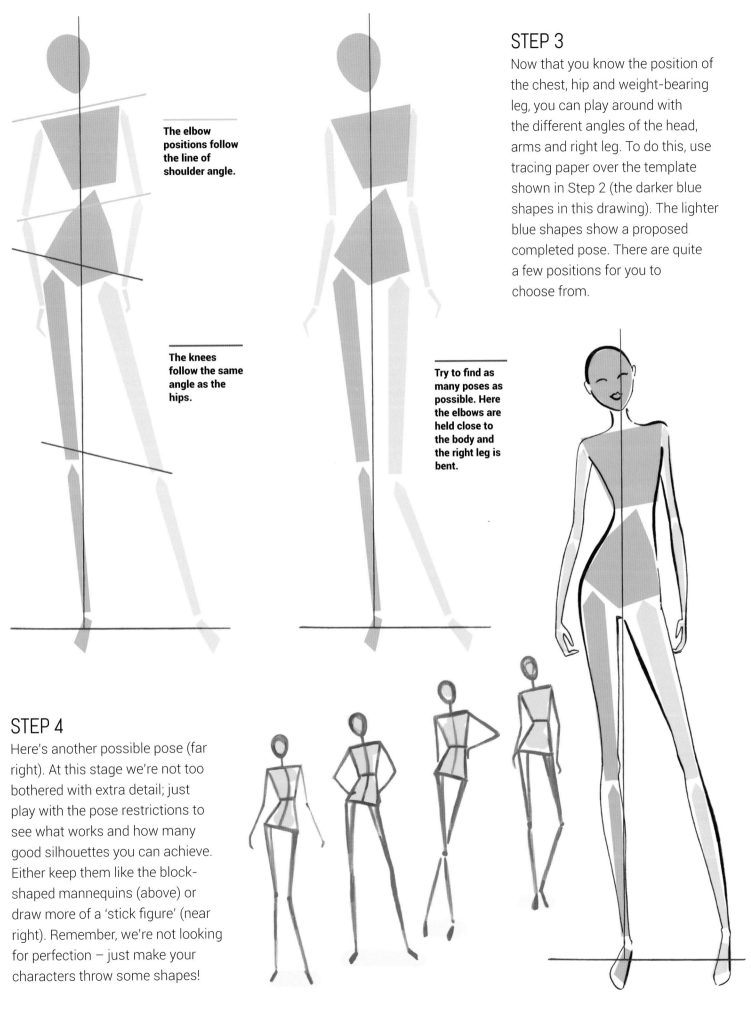

The elbow positions follow the line of shoulder angle.

The knees follow the same angle as the hips.

STEP 3

Now that you know the position of the chest, hip and weight-bearing leg, you can play around with the different angles of the head, arms and right leg. To do this, use tracing paper over the template shown in Step 2 (the darker blue shapes in this drawing). The lighter blue shapes show a proposed completed pose. There are quite a few positions for you to choose from.

Try to find as many poses as possible. Here the elbows are held close to the body and the right leg is bent.

STEP 4

Here's another possible pose (far right). At this stage we're not too bothered with extra detail; just play with the pose restrictions to see what works and how many good silhouettes you can achieve. Either keep them like the block-shaped mannequins (above) or draw more of a 'stick figure' (near right). Remember, we're not looking for perfection – just make your characters throw some shapes!

WALKING WOMAN POSE

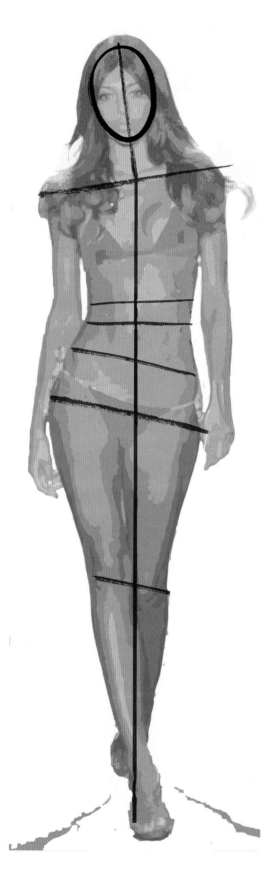

To draw this pose, find a photo of a model walking – runway swimwear shots are good as they show the full female form. They also give an idea of the physique that's in fashion. Whatever the build, be it super-skinny or more muscular and sporty, the model should have a good overall proportion to show off the clothes to their best advantage.

When you draw, make sure that one leg is completely straight (this will be the load-bearing leg) and positioned directly below the pit of the neck, where your balance line will start. The other leg will be lifted up, so the positioning of this is less important.

STEP 1

Start with your photo reference, cutting it out and sticking it down on the paper. If the model has her hair over her shoulders it will make it difficult to see the angle of the shoulder line, so look at the hips and draw the opposite angle for the shoulders. Make sure the figure is slightly oblique, but square on so there is no foreshortening. Place a sheet of tracing paper over the image and draw the angle of the head and neck and then the balance line, straight to the ground from the pit of the neck. The load-bearing leg should intersect this line. Draw in the angle of the shoulders, the bottom of the ribcage, the waist, the top of the hip and low hip and the position of the knees. Block in a rough shape for the feet.

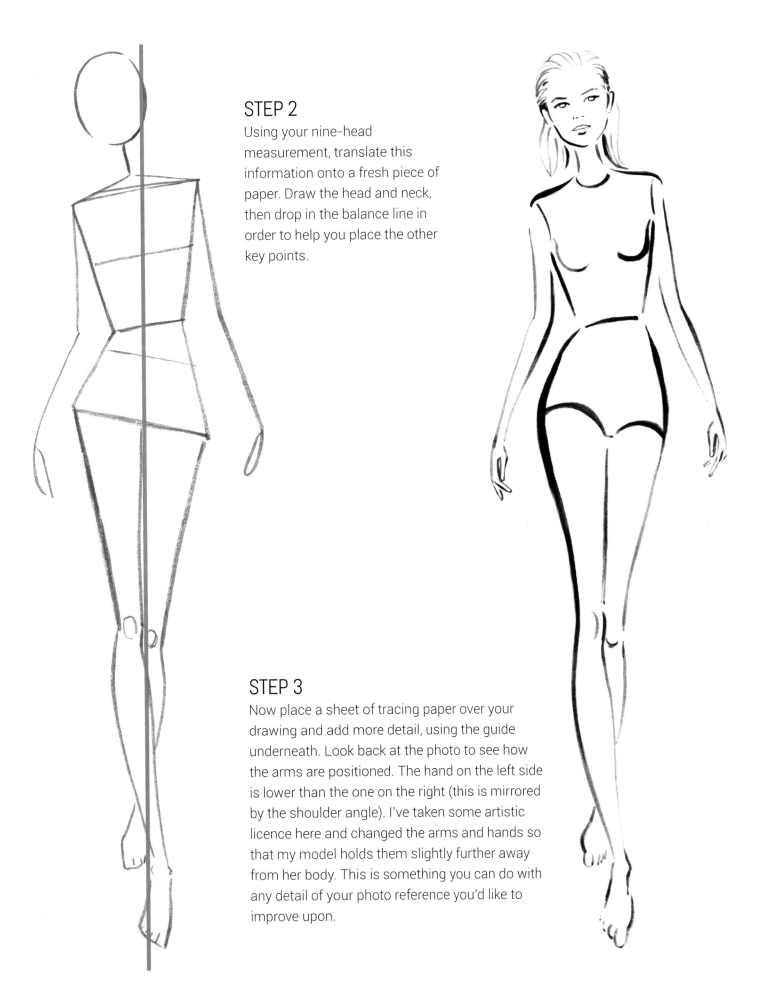

STEP 2

Using your nine-head measurement, translate this information onto a fresh piece of paper. Draw the head and neck, then drop in the balance line in order to help you place the other key points.

STEP 3

Now place a sheet of tracing paper over your drawing and add more detail, using the guide underneath. Look back at the photo to see how the arms are positioned. The hand on the left side is lower than the one on the right (this is mirrored by the shoulder angle). I've taken some artistic licence here and changed the arms and hands so that my model holds them slightly further away from her body. This is something you can do with any detail of your photo reference you'd like to improve upon.

THREE-QUARTER POSE

STEP 1

Roughly draw your head and neck and drop in the balance line. Add the shoulder, hip and knee angle lines (shown in red) and make sure they correspond correctly. Then draw in the body's centre front (blue dotted line); this will show how much more of the side nearest the viewer you'll see with the three-quarter pose and will help when you are working out the garment details.

STEP 2

Take a third off the width of the shoulder line where you want the model to turn away from you. Do the same with the hip line on that side. See how the centre front line bends as the body turns. Draw in the bust, which on the turned-away side is seen in profile.

Here the high-hip figure is straight on. Draw in the centre front (dotted blue line).

Here is the same figure at a three-quarter angle. The left side of the body is foreshortened, so appears smaller. Draw in the centre front, from the neck, through the sternum and belly button and finishing at the crotch. Notice how it curves at this angle.

Patterned coat in three-quarter pose

STEP 1

In this example, the model is turned in the opposite direction, so the measurements of the first pose are reversed.

STEP 2

Draw in the garment, in this case an oversized coat. Use the centre line as your guide for drawing the coat's centre front.

STEP 3

The coat has a complicated chevron pattern/weave, so work out the structure of this first in pencil.

STEP 4

I decided to render the coat in chisel-tip markers, using the pencil drawing in Step 3 as a guide. The blocky rendition could work as a finished drawing, just with the addition of shoe detail, but I wanted a more finished look.

STEP 5

Using fine-tip marker pens, I added texture to the coat and gave the model facial features. A couple of definition lines down the left side helped to anchor the figure.

MOVEMENT POSES

Fashion illustrations work best when they have a lovely natural flow that leads the eye and complements the garment being drawn. Most illustration poses fall into the following shapes: I, S, T, A and diamond.

Look at your reference fashion poses for inspiration. Take photocopies and draw over the images with marker pen, trying to follow the flow of the figure's movement. Is it all in one direction, straight down or at an angle? Does the figure curve with a sinuously arched back, with a change of direction in the angle of the hips? Do the arms just hang down at the sides or do they help to emphasize an area of interest on the outfit, or give character to the figure? Could you improve on the photo pose?

Ultimate dress for after-work drinks

Perfect frills for sitting and gossiping

I shape 1

The I shape (left) is a static, classic column pose which doesn't create much drama. It is left to the garment to grab the attention. If the outfit has lots of horizontal lines or a strange, extreme shape, then the stillness of this pose would be perfect to show it off.

I shape 2

This example of the 'I' pose (right) shows that you don't need lots of drama to create a sweet and arresting image. The clothes are very simple and young, and the pose helps to convey this mood perfectly.

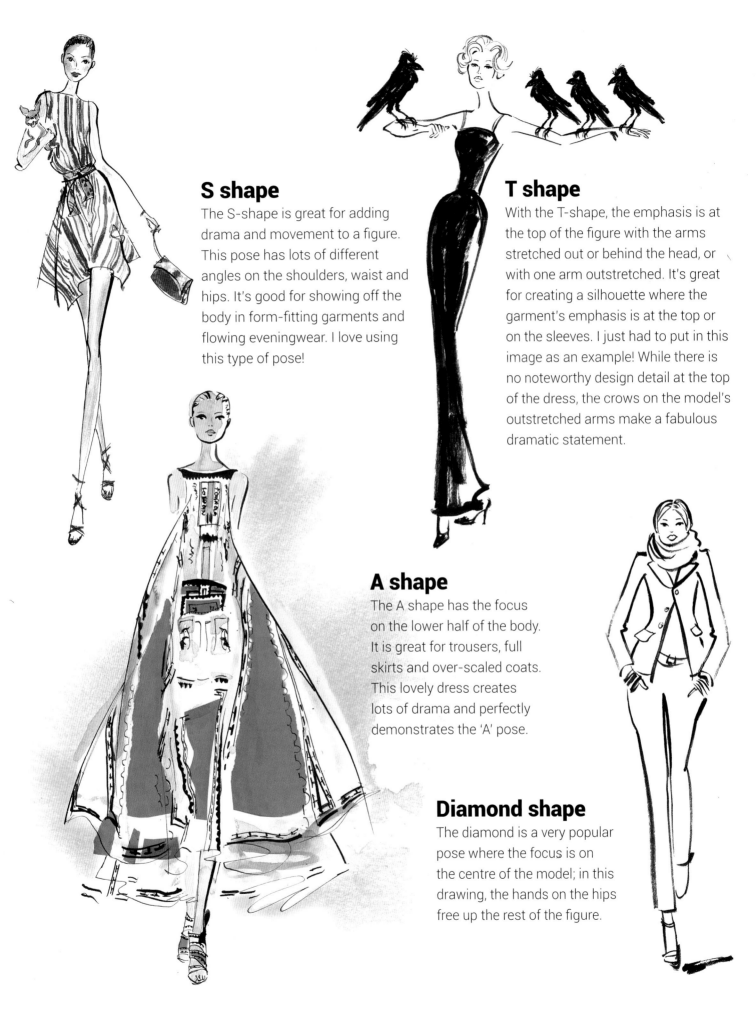

S shape

The S-shape is great for adding drama and movement to a figure. This pose has lots of different angles on the shoulders, waist and hips. It's good for showing off the body in form-fitting garments and flowing eveningwear. I love using this type of pose!

T shape

With the T-shape, the emphasis is at the top of the figure with the arms stretched out or behind the head, or with one arm outstretched. It's great for creating a silhouette where the garment's emphasis is at the top or on the sleeves. I just had to put in this image as an example! While there is no noteworthy design detail at the top of the dress, the crows on the model's outstretched arms make a fabulous dramatic statement.

A shape

The A shape has the focus on the lower half of the body. It is great for trousers, full skirts and over-scaled coats. This lovely dress creates lots of drama and perfectly demonstrates the 'A' pose.

Diamond shape

The diamond is a very popular pose where the focus is on the centre of the model; in this drawing, the hands on the hips free up the rest of the figure.

MALE FIGURES AND POSES

The drawing of male models seldom comes up in a commission. Consequently it can be a refreshing and enjoyable challenge. With men, there are fewer constraints on styling, so detail can be added for a more characterful, exaggerated look. Men's heads are more angular than women's, with stronger jawlines; this means that straight lines can be used to convey the features. I find that clients often ask for male models to be twice the size of females, insisting they have large shoulders, tiny waists and hips, thick necks and chiselled, square jaws – like something out of 50s action comics! In reality, the differences between the sexes are considerably less cartoonish and extreme.

Checklist for drawing the male figure
* ★ Head bigger than for the female figure
* ★ Neck thicker in relation to the shoulders
* ★ Shoulders wider, more angle on the trapezius muscle
* ★ Arm muscles more defined
* ★ Hands squarer, fingers blunter
* ★ Waist wider, lower torso tapering to hips (no curve)
* ★ Hips narrower, less movement in the hip and shoulder angles
* ★ Legs thicker, muscles more defined
* ★ Knees more prominent
* ★ Calves and ankles more angular

Remember, if the style of your female characters is gangly and awkward, then try to follow the same aesthetic with your male characters' proportions. Try making the males slightly taller and broader-shouldered. This will maintain the status quo without losing character or making them overwhelmed by bulk. Men have slightly larger heads proportionately, so bear this in mind when using this as the measuring unit for your figures.

Men tend to have more prominent muscles, wider shoulders and chests, longer torsos with a dropped waist and narrower hips – but you should avoid adding bulk for the sake of it.

Regarding poses, the standard women's high-hip pose is less obvious in the men's version. I've drawn it here so you can see how it works. The hip angle is less extreme (in a standing pose, a man's spine has less of an 'S' curve than a woman's), so there isn't so much contrast between hip and shoulder angles. The male head tends naturally to follow the angle of the shoulders. The high-hip pose is used a lot more for women than for men; it is thought more 'masculine' for a man to stand with legs apart and weight evenly distributed (which, in my opinion, reduces the range of poses significantly and can be boring). One way to be a bit freer is to include more action and drama in some of the poses. It's a good idea to shake up the image (especially if it's sportswear related) by having your model jumping or running.

Straight-on pose

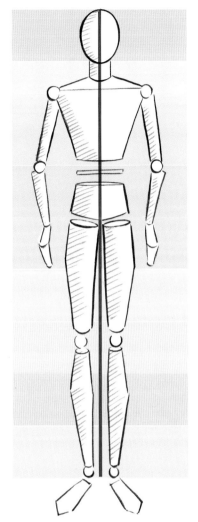 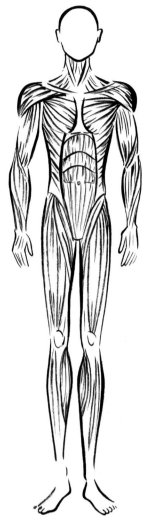  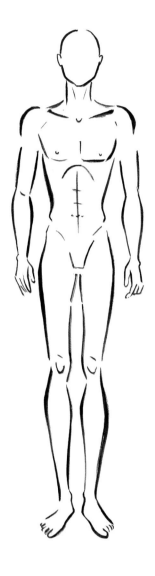

STEP 1
Draw the balance line and measure down in 4cm (1.5in) sections (nine in total). Draw an oval for the head in the first section and then follow the measurements in the diagram for the remaining body parts. The ideal silhouette is big shoulders and small waist and hips. Thighs and calves are less curvy than for the female.

STEP 2
This drawing shows you the muscles under the skin. The biggest difference from the female form is the build-up of muscle on the shoulders, but in general the muscles are more visible on the male form. Shoulder width is around 2 heads and the waist is 1.25 heads.

STEP 3
Use the muscle guide to add more form to your basic template shape. For example, look at the shoulder and trapezius lines in my version. Add this definition quite roughly, using lots of straight lines. Drop the crotch line on the male further down the leg.

STEP 4
Now trace over your artwork and draw a more detailed realistic figure. If in doubt, refer to photos of swimwear models for guidance.

WALKING MAN POSE

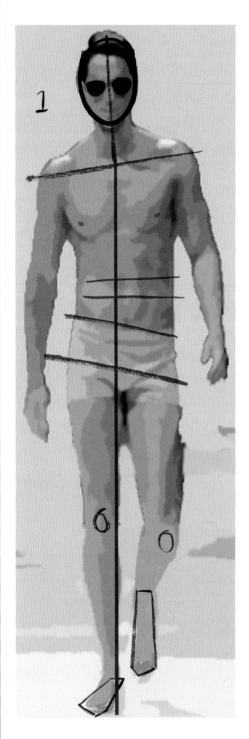

For this pose, find a photo of a man walking – again, runway swimwear is good as it will show a model with an athletic body and give an idea of current trends.

You Will Need
* male swimwear photo
* smooth paper
* HB and B pencils
* ruler
* fine-tip marker pens in black and red
* tracing paper

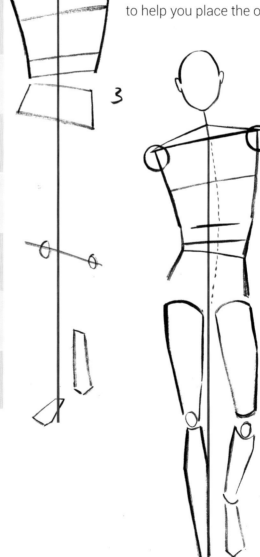

STEP 2

Using your nine-head measurement, translate this information onto a fresh piece of paper. Draw the head and neck, then drop in the balance line to help you place the other key points.

STEP 3

Draw the trapeze line of the shoulders and two circles to give you a rough idea of the muscles covering the shoulders. The red dotted line shows the angle of the centre front. Sketch in the legs using basic cylinder shapes. As with the walking woman pose, make sure the load-bearing leg is straight and positioned directly below the pit of the neck.

STEP 1

Start with your photo reference. Make sure the figure is turned slightly, but square-on so that there is no foreshortening. Trace the figure or draw straight onto it. Draw in the balance line and the other angles, following the instructions on pages 28–9.

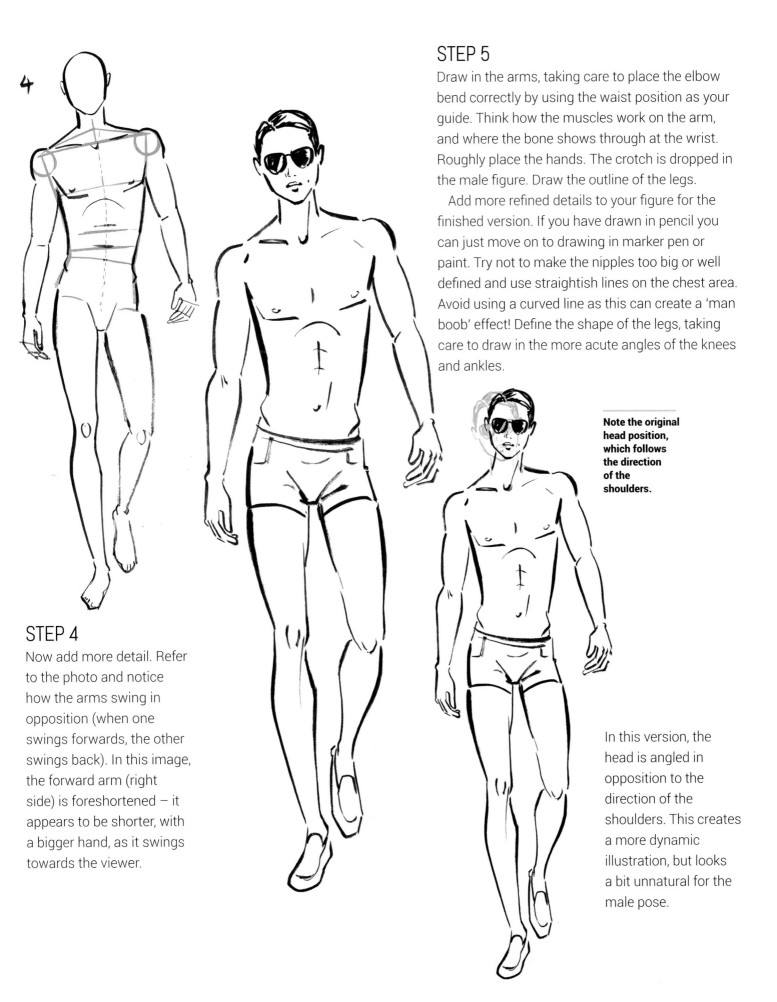

STEP 5

Draw in the arms, taking care to place the elbow bend correctly by using the waist position as your guide. Think how the muscles work on the arm, and where the bone shows through at the wrist. Roughly place the hands. The crotch is dropped in the male figure. Draw the outline of the legs.

Add more refined details to your figure for the finished version. If you have drawn in pencil you can just move on to drawing in marker pen or paint. Try not to make the nipples too big or well defined and use straightish lines on the chest area. Avoid using a curved line as this can create a 'man boob' effect! Define the shape of the legs, taking care to draw in the more acute angles of the knees and ankles.

Note the original head position, which follows the direction of the shoulders.

In this version, the head is angled in opposition to the direction of the shoulders. This creates a more dynamic illustration, but looks a bit unnatural for the male pose.

STEP 4

Now add more detail. Refer to the photo and notice how the arms swing in opposition (when one swings forwards, the other swings back). In this image, the forward arm (right side) is foreshortened – it appears to be shorter, with a bigger hand, as it swings towards the viewer.

MEN'S MOVEMENT POSES

When drawing men in motion, the temptation is to go for the 'testosterone pose' – for example, action men playing baseball, boxing, wrestling, diving, gymnastics and so on. All of these are great for creating original, frenetic poses. Contemporary dance is another good source of strange, physical poses that really push the body to its limits.

Rock-star pose

Dance-inspired movements

One trick that photographers use is to get models to jump straight up in the air. This is not something I'd recommend in your drawings, as it can give your characters an odd, unworldly feel. Try looking at comics for really interesting angles, especially *anime* comics, which are often drawn by very good artists. There are many photographic reference books you can use to find action poses.

**Basket-ball
action poses**

However, be careful if your brief is to illustrate certain garments because you don't want them to get lost in your extravagant poses – always keep in mind the clothing you want to represent. The more complicated the pose, the more extreme the foreshortening will be to the limbs. This is something I'm never that happy with; I'd rather spend time drawing a great garment than wondering if the left arm looks stubby compared to the right.

TWEEN FIGURES AND POSES

Children aged between ten and thirteen should be drawn with lots of attitude, as they are on the cusp of adolescence. They have a unique look that takes practice to perfect. To begin with, it can be difficult not to make them look like small adults.

Follow this basic template to create your tween boy and girl characters.

There are a few rules to help you achieve a young face. Look at the shaded blue artwork: this shows how tweens have prominent, rounded foreheads. The bridge of the nose hasn't fully developed and the cheeks are rounder and softer than an adult's. Try shading in one side of the face from the top of the forehead to the temple; then shade in the area between the eyes to show a slight hollow. Shade in a soft cheek. Make the eyebrows fine and not too big. Don't draw in the bridge of the nose – just draw the nostrils.

Using the template above as your starting point, start to add character. I like to make the ears stick out a bit, as it illustrates this sometimes awkward age before the tweens have grown into their features in early adulthood. I love giving boy characters scruffy hair and cheeky grins and girl characters a more groomed style, with either a defiant gaze or a more 'pink princess' expression with lots of accessories.

If the character you've drawn still looks too old, try moving the features lower down the face – this should help make him or her look younger. Big accessories (hair bands, bracelets and so on) and quirky hairstyles on girls will add cuteness. Avoid earrings, fine necklaces and makeup, especially strong colour on the lips, as these are ageing.

Seven-head tween girl figure

This tween girl is aged between eleven and fourteen. Her head is more or less fully grown, but her body and limbs are less well-developed. Often this is illustrated with oversized heads, short, thick, shapeless trunks and thin limbs, all making a gangly look. The waist is high and the body quite cylindrical, with a slight curve to the hip. The template is seven heads high; be careful not to elongate the figure as it will instantly make her look older. If you want to draw a younger child of, say, seven or eight years, knock a head off the height and adjust the proportions.

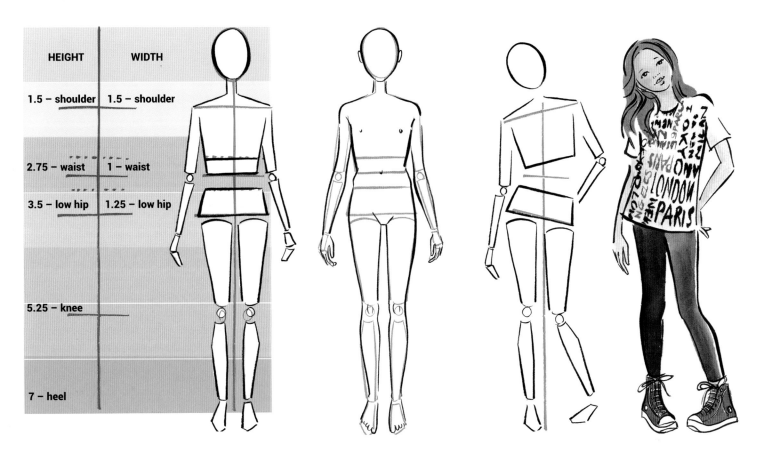

HEIGHT	WIDTH
1.5 – shoulder	1.5 – shoulder
2.75 – waist	1 – waist
3.5 – low hip	1.25 – low hip
5.25 – knee	
7 – heel	

STEP 1
Mark in the balance line and measure down the shoulder, waist and so on. Measure the widths of the body using the head unit as your guide. Draw in the blocked areas of the body.

STEP 2
Trace over the blocked-in template and draw a more rounded, detailed outline.

STEP 3
Here I've taken the basic template and moved the shoulder to a more severe angle. This means the hips move in the opposite angle and the leg position becomes more interesting.

STEP 4
I've added more detail and character to the pose, drawing the facial features as explained opposite. The stance portrays coyness and coolness and the pigeon toes and head tilt help to make her look young and give her attitude.

Seven-head tween boy figure

The measurements for the tween boy are very similar to those of the girl. The only differences are a slightly longer torso, so the waist is dropped, and less curvy hips. The pose I've drawn is a bit tricky, as the straight arms push up the shoulders unnaturally, but I think it's a lovely 'cool kid' pose!

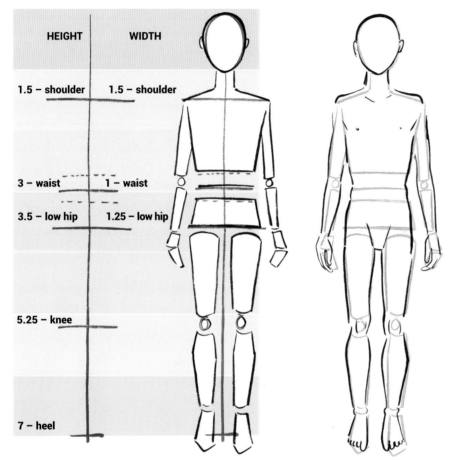

HEIGHT	WIDTH
1.5 – shoulder	1.5 – shoulder
3 – waist	1 – waist
3.5 – low hip	1.25 – low hip
5.25 – knee	
7 – heel	

STEP 1
Draw in the balance line and work out the widths of the various parts of the body.

STEP 2
Draw in the boxy body areas, following the measurements marked out.

The elbow joint is roughly at waist height, the wrist at low hip height and the fingers end at around 4.25 height.

STEP 3
Draw in a more accurate body shape and adjust to suit your ideas.

STEP 4
Here I've gone back to the box shapes and made the figure more dymanic, with an attitude stance.

STEP 5
This boy has long, floppy hair. I like boy images to have messy, sticking-out hair to give an unruly quality. If you want your character to look younger, the features should be more squashed into the lower half of the face shape.

BALANCE AND DETAIL

Now that you know how to draw a range of poses, we'll tackle a bit more detail.

In my drawing on the right, for the sake of ease, the head is directly over the load-bearing foot to help ground my figure. As we've already seen, the load-bearing leg is always straight. Here the model is standing with her legs apart. This can mean a more even distribution of weight, but in this case the leg on the left is set wide, giving an 'S' shape to the form.

Heads should be stylized in the same manner as the body. Remember, the image is not likely to be used very big, so not too much information needs to be added. Look at the work of other illustrators and see what they choose to leave out; it can make the difference between an average illustration and a strong one.

Regarding the hair, it is best to keep it simple. Don't try to show individual hairs, as your art will start to look prissy. Try to think what sort of woman would be wearing the outfit and what her attitude might be. In this pose, she is smart day casual, so hair tied back in a ponytail helps to convey the right feel of sporty, relaxed, edgy, high fashion. Look through fashion magazines for other ideas of high-fashion looks.

EYE LEVEL

It's important to consider the eye level of your pose. To find out what this means, look at your photo references and tear sheets and analyse the angle from which the photographer took the picture.

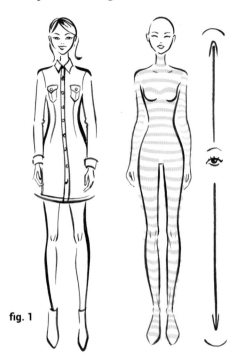

fig. 1

fig. 2

fig. 3

Most photos are taken on a tripod at hip height (fig. 1) because this is the most natural way to view a figure and gives the best proportion, without distortion. Most fashion illustrators use this angle, believing it is the most natural for both the drawer and the viewer.

Sometimes the photographer may be lying on the floor, looking up at the model (fig. 2). This will give the illusion of longer legs and a smaller head. The features that are close to the viewer will appear bigger and those that are further away will seem smaller.

Occasionally the photographer may use a high shot, taken from above the model (fig. 3), so that you see the top of the head. In this case, the body will be greatly foreshortened.

If you look at fashion advertising you will notice that a lot of models are shot from a low level. This (together with Photoshop, of course!) not only makes the legs appear longer, but also gives the feel of an iconic, classic figure. It creates the illusion that the model is raised up and suggests that you are revering their higher status (think 'Versace goddess').

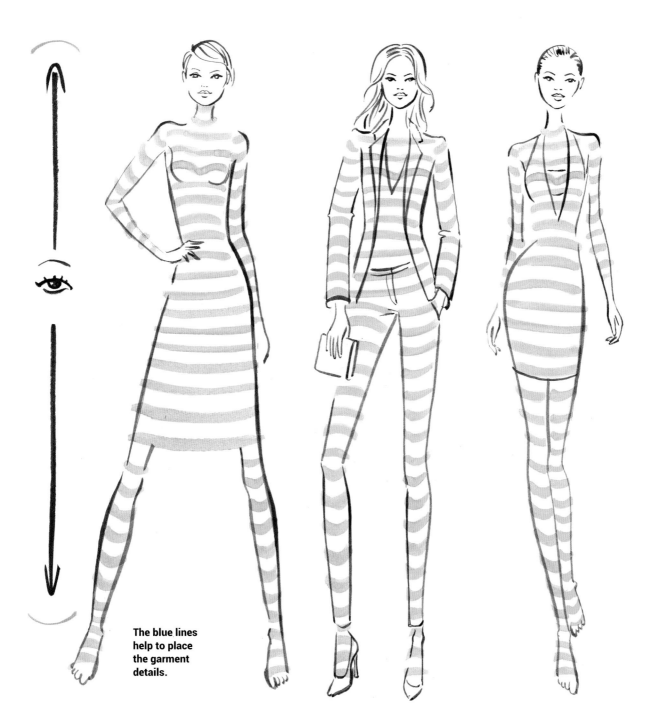

The blue lines help to place the garment details.

Drawing in contour lines on your model helps when it comes to placing garment details. Here I've shown the most usual hip-height angle for drawing the body; this is the easiest from which to get the proportions right (no pesky foreshortening!) I've drawn the contours in blue – see how the curves alter according to the eye level. The contour line at eye level (the hip) is shown as a straight line across the body. Gradually the curve increases in opposite directions the higher up and the further down it goes. Contour lines are a great guide for working out hemlines, pockets, waistlines, sleeves, stripes, checks and plaids.

POSE – TRACING METHOD 1

Now that you have absorbed the rules for measurements and angles, try using this tracing method to turn a reference pose into a fashion-proportioned figure. This is good if you enjoy cutting out and sticking, and like having some freedom to invent and refine your proportions.

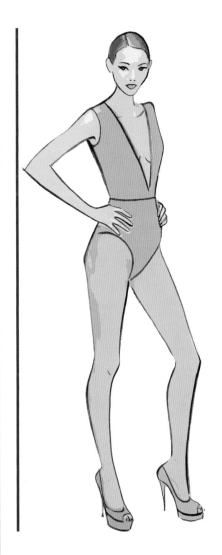

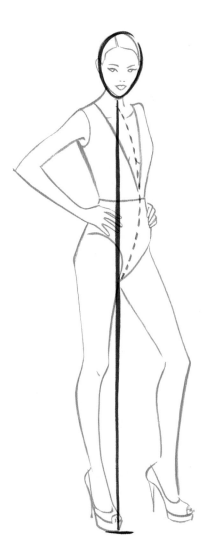

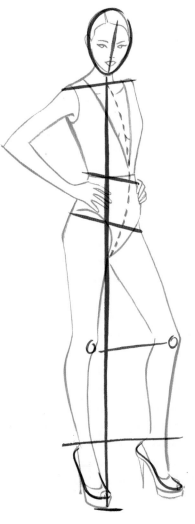

STEP 1

It's best to start with a simple high-hipped pose, maybe with the figure turned slightly to the side so that you can practise foreshortening. Cut out and stick your reference image in place and use a ruler to draw a vertical line next to it. Place your tracing paper over the figure, making sure it is securely fixed with the edge perpendicular to the vertical line.

STEP 2

Draw the balance line from the middle of the neck, between the shoulders, down to the floor. The load-bearing leg should be parallel with this line. Mark in the centre front of the body with a dotted line, from the pit of the neck, through the sternum and belly button, ending at the crotch.

STEP 3

Mark in the angles of the shoulders, waist and hip. Draw in the location and angles of the knees, feet and head.

STEP 4

Now it's time to transfer this information to your fashion figure scale. Using the nine-head scale, cut the figure up at the shoulder, waist, hip, knee and ankle angles and stick these pieces down next to the relevant points on the nine-head figure scale.

STEP 5

Once you have stuck down all the sections, take a clean sheet of tracing paper or plain paper if you are using a lightbox (on a sunny day you can tape your image to a window and use it the same way as a lightbox). Draw in the head, torso and legs of your fashion figure as freely as you can, using the sketched guide underneath. Referring to the original photo, sketch in the remaining features, the hands and the arms.

POSE – TRACING METHOD 2

This method saves you from going through the whole measuring process used in some of the other proportion methods shown in this book. It will appeal to the more wary illustrator, as the use of the underdrawing guide ensures that the figure is accurate.

Choose the photo you want to use as a guide. This can either be the design of a garment you want to draw or a great body and pose, or both of these things. This method is really useful if you need to draw stripes or checks that are reacting to the shape of the body.

For this example, I've used a fitted, checked coat. I hate drawing this kind of garment because of the rigid vertical and horizontal lines which need to be adhered to. This method helps you keep the correct angles while retaining some looseness and fluidity in the drawing. Don't draw in every single check, just add in an impression of the overall pattern. The finished figure is only about a head's length taller than the original drawing, but it seems a lot more than that because of the narrowing of the shoulders, waist and limbs. This is done gradually so that the dimensions remain true to the original photo reference.

STEP 1
Place a piece of photocopy paper or several layers of tracing paper over the image and tape down. You need to be able to see the reference photo, but not to do a traced copy – remember, this is just a guide. Draw in the main features you want to capture. For example, do you want the head to be straight or tilted to one side? What angle are the shoulders at? Where do the arms finish in relation to each other and where do they rest on the body or garment? Which leg is carrying the weight? In a walking pose, the weight placement can be tricky; the camera may capture the moment when the weight is shifting from one leg to the other. Here it is firmly placed on the left leg, as backed up by the hip and shoulder angles.

STEP 2
Place a further sheet of paper over the drawn image and photograph. You may wish to add in the check detail at this point, so that you can see the angles of the checks on different parts of the body. You can see the reference guide in grey behind the new

black version. At this point, I'm refining and picking out the parts of the figure and garment I wish to exaggerate. In this case, I love the prim collar and shoulder-line, the nipped-in waist and oversized sleeve cuffs. I've tried to exaggerate these elements to create more impact. If you are not happy with your drawing, just keep making corrections until you have an image you are satisfied with. The way you are creating the images should allow you to feel secure and relaxed, which will be evident in the drawings.

STEP 3
Now focus on gradually exaggerating the body length. The image is starting to look more streamlined and less bulky on the arms. This makes the cuffs seem more pronounced.

STEP 4
I started to lengthen the legs in Step 3. Here I lengthened them further until I was satisfied with the dimensions.

STEP 5
Draw in the black line and add colour. I placed the second reference guide with the drawn-in checks under this drawing so I could redraw my checks in a stretchy style. I added shadow to the face and legs, leaving some areas white.

CHANCE POSE

I love this sketch I did of a 'cool guy' on the street and feel that the proportions work well, even though they are not anatomically accurate. This chance pose demonstrates a quick way of dissecting proportions and transferring them to your new sketches. Tricks like this will give your portfolio cohesion.

To find your personal, preferred way of proportioning your fashion illustration, take a look through the figure drawings in your sketchbooks. They don't necessarily need to be fashion sketches; just pick out ones you think look right and seem to work. In my example, I've used a quick sketch I did of a guy on the street in charcoal pencil, which I coloured in later with marker pen. Measure the head of your sketchbook figure, using a ruler or finger or mark on a separate piece of paper, and calculate how many head lengths account for the total height. On my example, it's 8.5 heads from the back of the heel to the top of the head.

The waist is three heads down, the hips are four. The crotch height is lower than in the female figure, so drop this by a third of a head (this also depends on what clothing your model is wearing – lots of men's fashion has the crotch dropped further than normal). The knees are around the halfway point between crotch and foot.

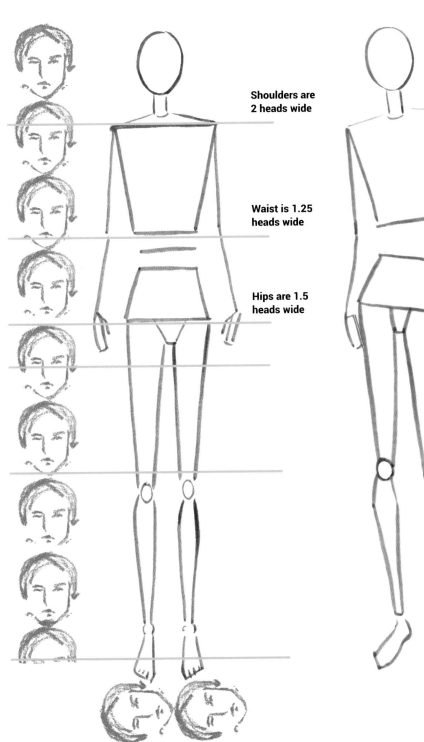

Shoulders are
2 heads wide

Waist is 1.25
heads wide

Hips are 1.5
heads wide

STEP 1

Draw up your basic body
template using the found
measurements.

STEP 2

Now you are ready to draw
the figure in the chance pose,
using your basic template as
a guide.

STEP 3

Draw a more detailed body on top
of this posed figure. As an extra
challenge, use different clothing
from the original sketch.

ILLUSTRATORS' CHART

This is just a bit of fun! It's my rendering of how different illustrators would interpret the figure and – guess what? – they are all successful in their own right.

I've taken typical drawings by seven fashion illustrators I admire, copied the proportions and drawn a version of each in their style. I've put them to scale to show how many times the head length fits into the body length. It's interesting to see the result. The only 'old school' illustrator here is René Gruau, whose figure is eight heads tall. The tallest model is by contemporary illustrator Arturo Elena, whose leggy model comes in at 10.5 heads high!

1. Ruben Toledo   **2. Bil Donovan**   **3. Mats Gustafson**

4. Fifi Lapin   5. Arturo Elena   6. David Downton   7. René Gruau

Chapter 4 FACES AND OTHER FEATURES

I love drawing faces. There is so much variety and you can alter them radically with very subtle changes. There are fashion trends in faces, just as there are in clothes, so it's worth checking to see what look is in and adapting your artwork to suit.

DRAWING FACES

First we'll look at the full-face view, which is less complicated than other angles and has no foreshortening. Faces vary greatly in features and proportion. We'll start with a generic shape which can be given more specific features once you've established the basics.

You Will Need
★ smooth paper
★ HB pencil
★ ruler
★ tracing paper
★ mirror

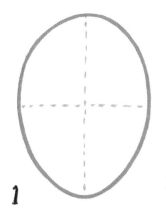

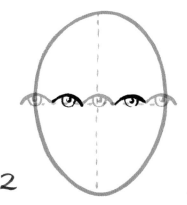

STEP 3
Draw in the hairline and two lines which radiate from the chin up past the outside edge of the eye. This a rough guide for the mouth and eyebrows.

STEP 1
Draw an oval, then draw a vertical and a horizontal line to divide the oval into four equal parts.

STEP 2
The eyes are located on the horizontal line. Think of them as almond-shaped and draw them as roughly one-fifth of the head width. Make sure they are one eye-width apart. If you want to be precise, there's half an eye-width space from the edge of the eye to the side of the head.

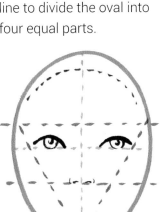

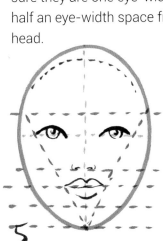

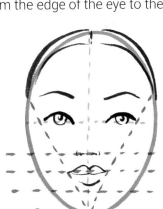

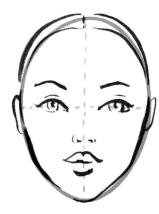

STEP 4
From the hairline down, divide the head horizontally into three. The nostrils are placed on the second line.

STEP 5
Divide the area between the nostrils and the chin into thirds. Draw the lips in the top and middle thirds, keeping them inside the diagonal lines placed earlier. This isn't an unbreakable rule; the mouth can be wider if you prefer.

STEP 6
Draw in the eyebrows on the first horizontal line. Draw in the hairline.

STEP 7
Draw the shape of the face, curving in slightly from the cheekbones. The tops of the ears are placed at eye level, while the bottoms of the ears are at nostril level. The face shape changes at mouth level for the jaw, which angles towards the chin. We'll talk more about face shape on the next page.

REFINING THE FACE SHAPE

Refining the face shape is a subtle art, and very subjective. This really will be showing the viewer the sort of character you want to be wearing your clothes.

You Will Need
★ smooth paper
★ HB pencil
★ ruler
★ range of marker pens in your chosen colours
★ tracing paper

In fashion drawing, a stylized version of the face is required, as too much detail can age the character. Generally not much detail is shown, especially for full-length poses; the eyes and the mouth are the main features. I tend not to draw much of the nose in a full-length image, just a hint of shadow under the tip or on one side of the bridge. You can experiment with a squarer jawline and high cheekbones, for a strong, commanding character, or try a small chin, big forehead and doe eyes for a waif-like model.

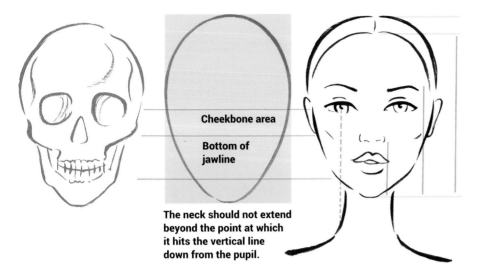

Cheekbone area

Bottom of jawline

The neck should not extend beyond the point at which it hits the vertical line down from the pupil.

Don't colour the entire face in a flesh tone – just colour down one side to create shading and depth.

STEP 1

Start by choosing a rectangular piece of paper with a 2:3 ratio. Draw in an egg shape, tapering at the bottom for the chin. Look at the skull image on the left. Studying the bones beneath will really help your understanding of the face when drawing the cheekbones and chin areas.

STEP 2

Draw in the vertical and horizontal lines to make the face symmetrical (see page 57) and place the features. Follow the curve of the cheekbone and jawline as seen on the skull, but moderate it so that the model doesn't look too gaunt. Decide how prominent you want the cheekbones to be; many fashion models have a heavily defined bone structure.

After drawing the cheekbone, which starts at eye level and curves in slightly until about nostril height, the outline returns to a line which tapers in to the jawbone. The start of this line is usually the level at which the lips meet. The lower you go past this point, the stronger the jawbone will look. This is useful when drawing men, but less so for female faces. In my drawings I tend to have the mouth level with the start of this line.

A long, slim neck is always a good foundation for the head. If you draw a line down from the outer edge of the iris of the eye, the neck should be parallel with this.

STEP 3

Start practising different looks based on interesting photo references from fashion magazines so that you get used to drawing quickly and building up a repertoire of personalities.

DRAWING THE FEATURES

The drawing of the eyes and mouth is important for giving your characters attitude. Remember to keep the angle of the head fairly simple to avoid awkward positionings.

Drawing the eyes

When drawing the eyes in close-up, show the iris in colour, but don't draw the whole round shape as this will give the face a startled look. You only see the whole iris when someone is frightened and staring 'wide-eyed' (think of all those old horror film posters!) The top eyelid looks best when resting on the pupil (the dark circle in the centre of the eye).

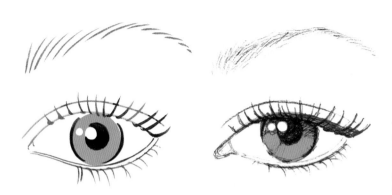

Here the eye looks startled because most of the iris is showing.

Here the iris is only three-quarters showing, veiled by the upper lid, making for a more natural effect.

The lower the point at which the top eyelid intersects the pupil, the sleeper or sexier the eye will look. Draw the eye as an almond shape, and flick out the outer corner of the top lash for a sophisticated look. Adding in the crease above the eye is useful when drawing older people as it gives them a hooded-eye look.

For a full-length pose, I tend to draw the eyes just as a top lash and a dark iris/pupil, unless asked for a specific eye colour by the client.

Drawing the mouth

Start with an elongated 'M' shape for the centre of the mouth, where the lips join. Add depth by darkening the outer corners. Draw the top lip, not too full, with a dip in the centre for the Cupid's bow. This is a matter of personal choice and can greatly influence the look. Draw the bottom lip fuller and bigger than the top lip, with a shadow underneath.

In the middle of the top lip is a circle of highlight. There are highlighted circles on the bottom lip, so that it looks fuller.

It is best not to draw the individual teeth as this can look sinister. However, there are illustrators who do, and do it very well. They tend to be very soft, detailed drawings – look out for the work of Garance Doré, for example.

Drawing noses

When drawing women, less is best for noses, often just a shadow down one side of the bridge. But if you want to get technical, the nose is composed of three circles – a bigger one in the middle for the tip and two smaller ones either side for the nostrils.

THE HEAD IN PROFILE

Profiles can be tricky to draw. It's important to learn the underlying structure of the head before you start. It's worth drawing your template, then placing a couple of layers of tracing paper over the top and testing out different profiles on these.

You Will Need
* smooth paper
* HB pencil
* ruler
* eraser
* tracing paper

The female head
For a feminine look, draw a rounded forehead. There is no eyebrow ridge, as seen on the male profile.

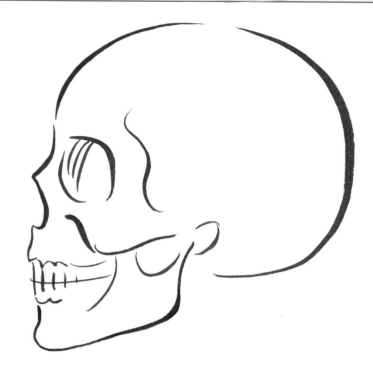

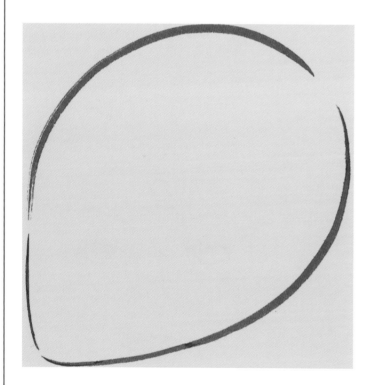

STEP 1
On a square piece of paper, draw an egg shape obliquely with a tapered end in the corner.

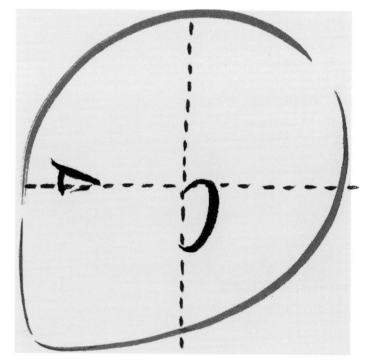

STEP 2
Draw a vertical and a horizontal line to meet in the middle of the square. This will help you determine the end of the jaw, and the ear and eye positions.

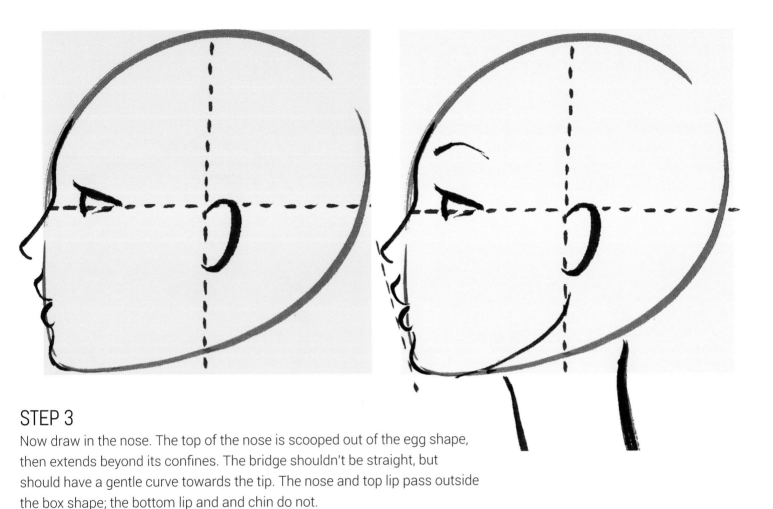

STEP 3

Now draw in the nose. The top of the nose is scooped out of the egg shape, then extends beyond its confines. The bridge shouldn't be straight, but should have a gentle curve towards the tip. The nose and top lip pass outside the box shape; the bottom lip and and chin do not.

STEP 4

Draw in the eyebrow, the rest of the jawline and the neck. Take a ruler and place it along the tip of the nose and chin (shown as a red dotted line). It is a sign of beauty, apparently, if the lips touch this line; if they don't, the nose or chin might be too prominent.

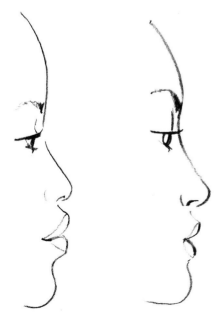

The best profiles have a gentle curve to them with the features not too far forwards. A mistake is to draw all the features in a vertical line; this makes the chin look very strong and gives the face a flat look.

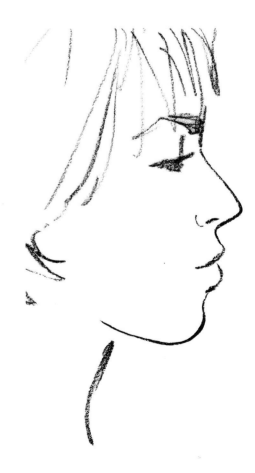

THE THREE-QUARTER HEAD

As a student this was always my favourite angle for drawing heads, showing lots of character in the strong eyebrows, pouting lips, razor-sharp cheekbones and long eyelashes. The eyes turn to meet your gaze – very Amazonian!

You Will Need

★ smooth paper
★ HB pencil
★ ruler
★ eraser
★ tracing paper

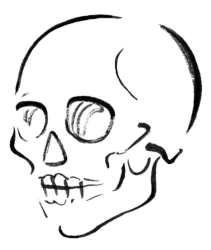

It helps to have a character in mind for your drawings. When designing a range, it is best to use one strong 'muse' rather than getting bogged down with a cast of characters.

Drawing the three-quarter head

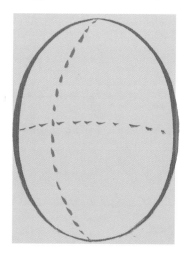

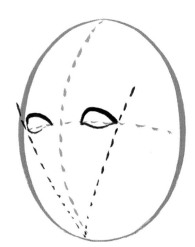

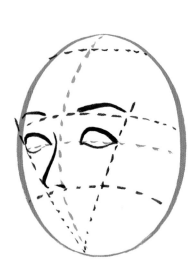

STEP 1

Start with an oval in a rectangular box. Mark the centre of the face. The face is turned to the left, so the features on this side will be foreshortened and occupy a smaller space. Also block halfway down the head. Both your lines should be curved, as they follow the oval's contours.

STEP 2

The point at which the lines cross is your guide to the space between the eyes. On the three-quarter head, this space measures about three-quarters of an eye width. As with the full frontal head, mark in the two diagonal lines radiating up from the chin to the outer corners of the eyes.

STEP 3

Mark in the hairline, then divide the rest of the oval into thirds. Mark the eyebrows in the first section and the nose in the second.

STEP 4

Divide the area beneath the nose into three equal sections. The first line is where the lips meet. Draw in the lips on either side of this line.

STEP 5

Now it's time to draw the facial outline. Beneath the eyebrow, the forehead curves into the eye socket and curves out again for the cheekbone. Then it tapers back in towards the chin, where it swells out again slightly for the point. On the side of the oval, draw in the ear from the top of the eyeline to nostril height; draw in the other side of the jawline from chin to ear, being careful not to make the line too heavy.

STEP 6

In this pose, the swell of the back of the head is more visible and the ears are enveloped in the overall outline of the head.

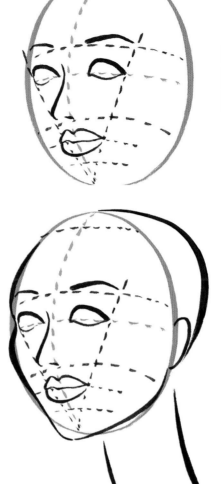
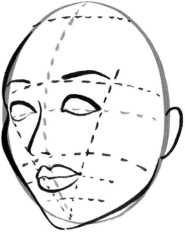

Use this guide to draw several heads, each with different looks, with tracing paper over the guide or on a lightbox. If you are comfortable using Photoshop, scan in this template and scale it up to the size needed for your figures. Use it as a guide or to check if existing drawings are correct.

Creating three-quarter features

The first eye I've drawn here is only slightly turned to the left. To draw the same eye in a three-quarter turn, look at the next drawing. The dotted red line shows the part of the eye that will be foreshortened (about a quarter) and the part which will not. Draw the right-hand side of the eye in the normal size, then fit the foreshortened side into the new contracted width.

The same principle applies to the lips and the nose. In the three-quarter pose, the bridge of the nose starts to become visible and may obscure the inner corner of the eye on the turned side of the head. It all depends on how strong you want the nose of your character to be. The nostril on the side of the face that is turned away from you becomes just a single mark. As a rough guide, the width of the nose should be the same as the distance between the eyes.

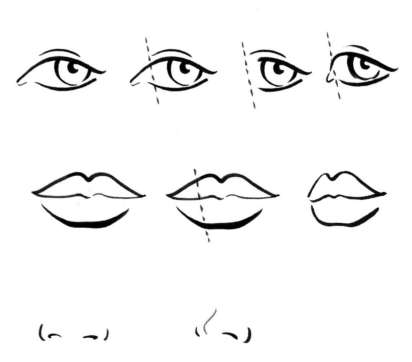

ARMS AND LEGS

Arms – fantasy/reality

Here you can see the difference between a fashion torso (fig. 1) and a normal torso (fig. 2). In fig. 1, the shoulder is more prominent and bony and the bust doesn't break the silhouette. The waist is more defined and the hip bone is prominent.

When the arm is bent (fig. 3), the lower inner arm is always curved and the lower outer arm is always straight.

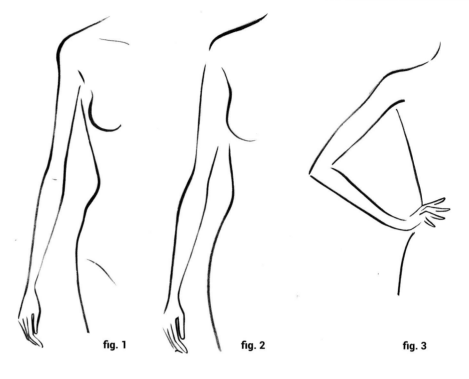

fig. 1   fig. 2   fig. 3

In the first drawing you can see the bone structure inside the leg, and where the bone is close to the surface at the knee and the ankle.

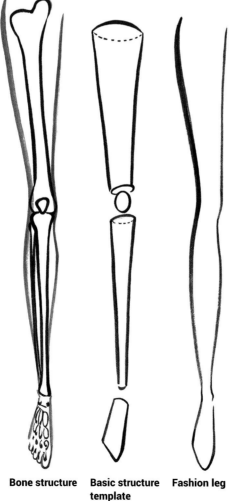

Bone structure   **Basic structure template**   **Fashion leg**

Legs – fantasy/reality

Here you can see the difference between a realistic leg and a fashion illustration leg. With the fantasy leg you'll notice that there is less curve on the outer thigh and no curve on the inside leg – it's just a straight line from crotch to knee. The fashion leg knee is smaller than the real knee; the outside calf starts with a higher curve and then straightens out to the ankle. The inside calf curves out from the knee, then curves gently inwards.

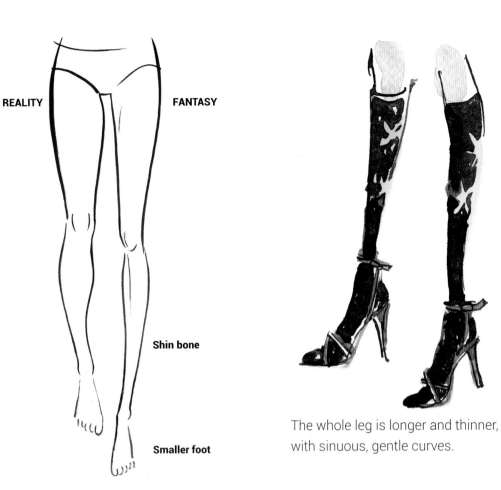

REALITY

FANTASY

Shin bone

Smaller foot

The whole leg is longer and thinner, with sinuous, gentle curves.

HANDS

Most people struggle to draw hands realistically. The complex structure of bone and muscle means there's a lot to contend with. I spent years putting my figures' hands in their pockets or behind their hips because I found hands difficult and wanted to get on with drawing the 'good bits' ! This might be fine for the beginner, but at some point you'll have to tackle them, just as I did.

You Will Need
* smooth paper
* HB and B1 pencil
* eraser
* mirror

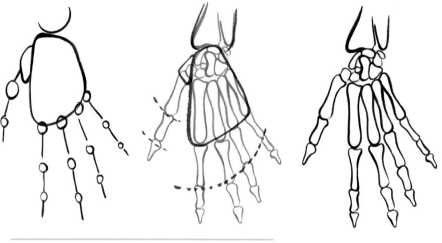

Start with basic shapes for the bones in the hand.

When illustrating the fashion figure, it's best to keep things simple. Overworked hands can draw the viewer's eye and risk becoming the main focus of the image, which is the last thing you want. Your hand is bigger than you think – you can cover your face, from chin to hairline, with one hand. In fashion illustration, clients tend to prefer a stylized, scaled-down version of the hands. But avoid making them too small – you're drawing a woman, not a Barbie doll.

You seldom see all five digits at once, so try not to be too clever with the hand positions as this can give your finished image a self-conscious look. While taking care not to draw a boneless 'hook' or 'rubber glove', don't spend too much time drawing each finger or you will end up with a bunch of bananas or a messy scrawl.

When drawing the full figure, don't waste time drawing the nails. This is only necessary in close-up images. The thumb is distinct from the other fingers. When a figure is standing in a relaxed pose, the thumb should be resting against the thigh facing the viewer. It's a good idea to use a mirror to check that the hand position feels comfortable and realistic. It's also useful for checking that the thumb is on the correct side of the palm!

Below are two realistic hands drawn from observation.

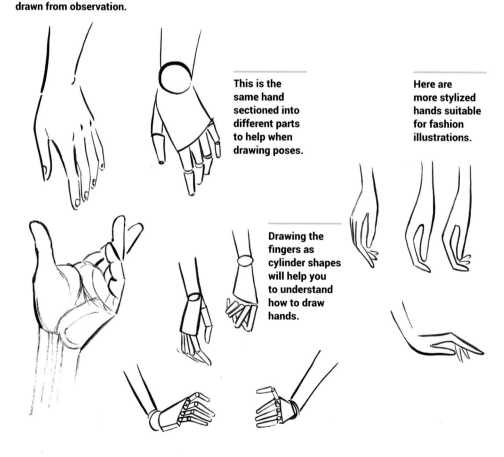

This is the same hand sectioned into different parts to help when drawing poses.

Drawing the fingers as cylinder shapes will help you to understand how to draw hands.

Here are more stylized hands suitable for fashion illustrations.

Building the hand

Look carefully at the bone structure of the hand and break it down into simple shapes.

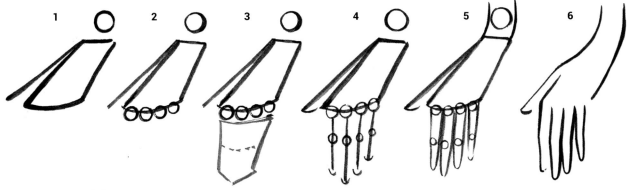

STEP 1

Draw a circle for the wrist and a rough oblong for the palm, making sure that the length is greater than the width and that the oblong widens towards the knuckles. This shape is also longer on the thumb side. Draw the thumb as a straight line fairly close to the palm.

STEP 2

Draw four circles for the knuckles. They should be on a curve going up towards the little finger and should fill the palm shape from one side to the other.

STEP 3

The red shape shows where I want to position the fingers. The shape becomes narrower to represent the fingers tapering. The middle finger is the longest point.

STEP 4

Draw lines for the fingers, marking the joints with circles and the ends of the fingers with half circles. The thumb finishes just below the knuckle.

STEP 5

Draw in the individual fingers. Make sure the fingertips are rounded and not too thin and pointed.

Alternative views

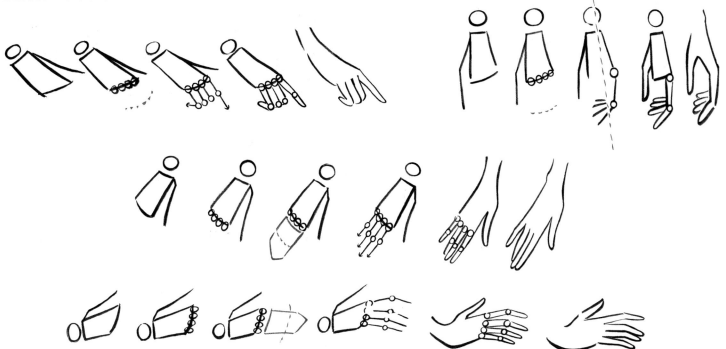

DRAWING HAIR

You Will Need
★ smooth paper
★ HB pencil
★ ruler
★ eraser
★ tracing paper

When illustrating a woman with a ponytail, many of us will draw a curved arch of forehead and then the hair, which makes the face look naive and unrealistic. As hairlines vary from person to person, I'm showing you a generic way to draw a head of hair.

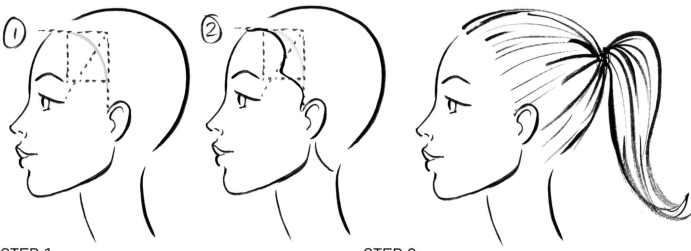

Full frontal hairline

STEP 1

Use the face template (page 57) to draw the face of your model. Mark in a vertical centre line and draw two vertical lines from the outer corners of the eyebrows to the top of the head. Join these with a horizontal line at the top. Mark a halfway point on the vertical lines to show where the temples are.

Profile hairline

STEP 2

The hairline follows the dotted line guide. Draw a slight downwards bump in the middle, then curve the line at each corner where it joins the vertical. Draw the line down to the temple mark. The line should be like a stretched 'M' shape. Now curve the line gently down and around the top of the ear.

STEP 1

Draw a horizontal line at the top of the brow, then draw a vertical line up from the ear to meet it. Join these two lines with a curve (shown in blue). Draw a diagonal from the eye to where the two lines meet, a vertical from the eyebrow to the horizontal, and a horizontal from the eyebrow to the vertical.

STEP 2

Starting at the top lefthand corner of the box, draw a curve with a peak (which should touch the diagonal line), then a further curve towards the ear. Add hairline in front of the ear. Draw a curve from the back of the ear to the top of the neck. Dip the line down a bit at the top of the hairline.

Three-quarter view

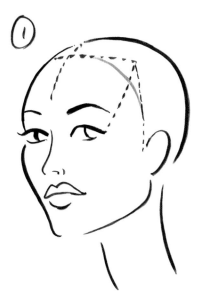
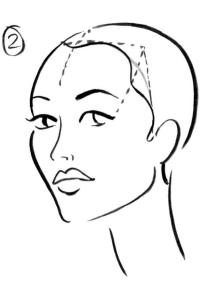

STEP 1

Mark in the centre, horizontal and vertical lines (up from the ear). Remember to curve these lines, because the head is rounded like a globe. Draw in the diagonal from the corner of the eye to where the lines meet. Draw in a curve connecting the horizontal and vertical lines (shown in blue).

STEP 2

Draw the middle part of the hairline that dips down on the forehead, then curve the line round the forehead and slowly towards a soft point at the temple (where it should touch the diagonal line). Now take the line down towards the ear and a bit in front of it.

Back view

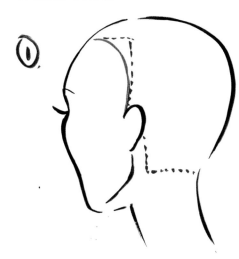
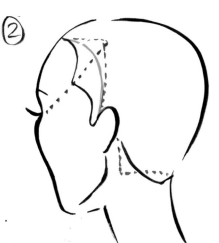

STEP 1

Draw a horizontal line at the hairline, a vertical line down to the ear and another from the back of the ear to the jawbone. Draw a horizontal line across the nape of the neck. Draw a curve connecting the horizontal and vertical lines.

STEP 2

Mark in the diagonal from the corner of the eye (where the eyelash is) to where the lines meet. Using this as your reference, mark halfway along for the temple. Draw a curve from the top of the hairline to the temple mark, then another curve towards the ear. Draw in the curve at the nape, dropping it lower than the dotted line, as shown.

Drawing tone

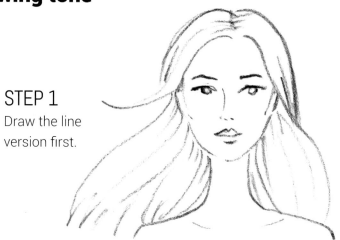

STEP 1
Draw the line version first.

You Will Need
- ★ smooth paper
- ★ HB pencil
- ★ charcoal pencil
- ★ range of pastels or coloured pencils, from light to dark

STEP 2
You can see where to add the darkest colour – at the roots, where the parting is, and around the ears, chin, neck and shoulders.

STEP 3
Here you can see where to add the lighter tone. Remember that most of it will be coloured over. Leave the highlighted areas white.

STEP 5
Then add your colour.

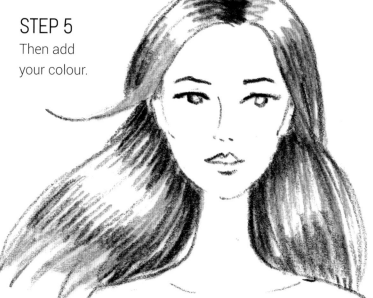

STEP 4
Now add the mid-tones – don't cover all the previous shading.

Different styles

1. In this pencil version, you can see the hair texture and direction it flows in. If your pencil lines are neat, you can just colour over them. Mine are messy, so I usually rub them out.

2. Hair produces a lot of reflective shine. On this type of style, where the hair falls down from the crown of the head, there will always be a highlight on either side of the head, near the top. Colour in the lightest shade of the hair, making sure your marks follow the direction of flow.

3. Add a mid-tone over most of your lighter shade, but leave some of it showing near the white highlights to give a graduated look.

4. Now add the darkest shade. This goes on the centre parting and the area behind the ear, chin, neck and where the hair falls behind the shoulders.

1. This pencil drawing shows a shorter hairstyle.

2. The model is dark blonde and has a heavy fringe, so the highlighted area is halfway down the fringe and extends around to the side of the head.

3. The fringe curls back in towards the eyebrows. Draw a darker area here to help make the head look three-dimensional.

4. Add darker tone to the middle of the top of the head and areas behind the ear and chin.

The highlights are different on this style. The hair is pushed back on top of the head, so it will appear darker at the roots and around the silhouette of the head, with a highlight in the middle.

Chapter 5 DRAWING FASHION

Now that you know how to create great poses, it's time to add some fashion garments. In this chapter we explore the effects of fabric quality, body shape, pose and gravity upon clothes and show how to render them.

FORM AND LINE

This full empire-line dress shows how the body underneath affects the line of the garment. The dress hangs from under the bust so the seamline is the same as the shoulder angle. The dress wants to hang in same direction as the shoulders, but the hips move in the opposite direction and push against the skirt on the right side, causing it to buckle (shown in red).

Drapes and folds

Draw a basic draped top with a cowl neckline.

Draw the soft folds of the neckline hanging over the chest area. The folds also affect the shoulderline, creating folds here too. Add these in, together with a slight fold at the waist.

Fabric types

Drapes and folds fall into three distinct groups: straight lines sometimes with a curve at one end; U-shaped lines (for soft fabrics such as silk); and short, broken, V-shaped lines (for crisp fabrics such as taffeta).

Draw your fabric lines.

Now add the tension lines and folds to suit the type of fabric you are using.

BLACK SUIT

Let's start with this classic slim black suit. Drawing black clothing presents certain challenges. If you draw it in solid black it can deaden the image and all detail may be lost. Try to represent the true black in perhaps 50 per cent of your illustration, then use a lighter shade for the rest so that the linework is visible. It shouldn't look too grey – practice will help you find the right combination.

STEP 1

Draw the outline. If you are using a brush to draw the details of the jacket, don't make the lines too thick. You need to leave space to create a margin in the next step.

STEP 2

Shade in the black with either marker pen or watercolour. Vary the depth of tone, and leave a margin of white at the edge so that detail isn't lost on the collar and hemline.

STEP 3

Add highlights in a soft grey to points of interest – collar, zip, waistband and so on. Add highlights from just one side to show the source of light and give a three-dimensional effect.

TROUSERS

This is a great template for starting your trouser designs, showing the waist, centre line and legs.

Wide-leg pants

STEP 1

Draw the basic shape of your wide-leg pants. Add a centre crease for the proportions. The bent leg hemline is slanted because the knee is pulling up that side.

STEP 2

Add creases (shown in blue). Draw creases radiating out from the crotch, mostly on the leg that is bent. The folds above the knee point down; the folds below point up.

STEP 3

Draw in the details using the previous image as your guide. The fabric on the hemline of the bent leg is pulled up, showing the back of the trouser leg and forming an 'S' or '?' shape.

Capri pants

STEP 1

You can see the basic capri pant shape in blue. The bent leg hemline slants up, as before.

STEP 2

When you've drawn the basic shape, draw in the fold lines on the trousers. Add creases to the side profile of the bent leg and back of the knee.

STEP 3

Add the detail to the top of the capri pants. The bent leg hemline slants up and the high hip swings to the right.

Classic straight pants

STEP 1
Draw your basic shape, remembering to make the hemline on the bent leg slant upwards.

STEP 2
Add folds to your shape (shown in blue). Notice the extra creases at the back of the knee.

STEP 3
Add the waistband – it's a dropped waist, so the curve is downwards. Add pocket details using the waistband as a guide.

Shorts

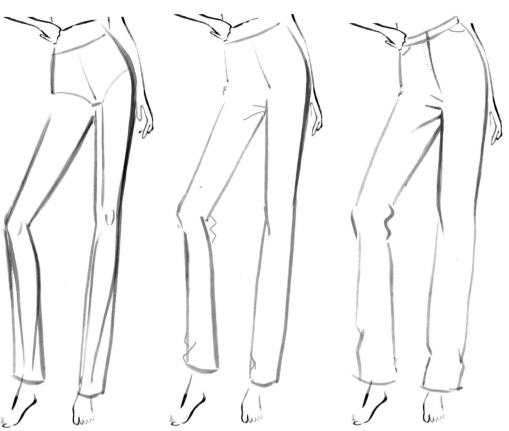

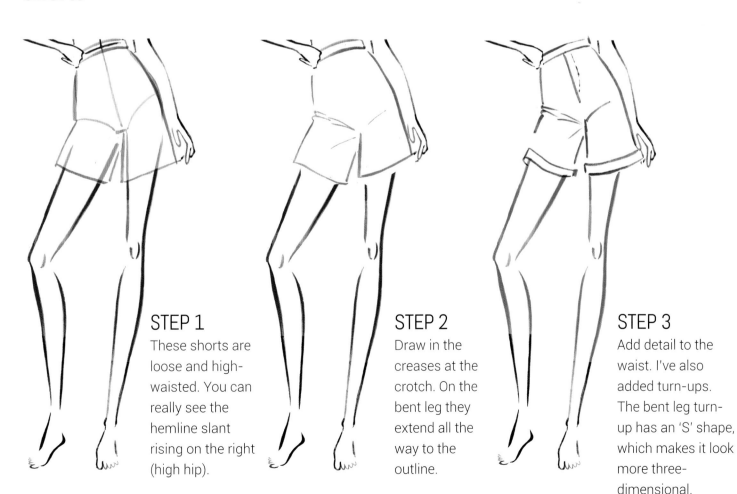

STEP 1
These shorts are loose and high-waisted. You can really see the hemline slant rising on the right (high hip).

STEP 2
Draw in the creases at the crotch. On the bent leg they extend all the way to the outline.

STEP 3
Add detail to the waist. I've also added turn-ups. The bent leg turn-up has an 'S' shape, which makes it look more three-dimensional.

SKIRTS

Here I've drawn three different types of skirt, showing how the pose, the body and gravity all affect the garments.

The four silhouette figures show where the garment reacts against the body and creates compression folds (shown as yellow circles). The second image shows a garment hanging from an unposed figure.

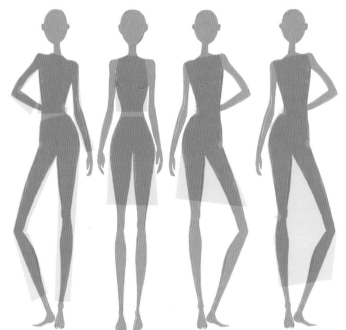

Short A-line skirt

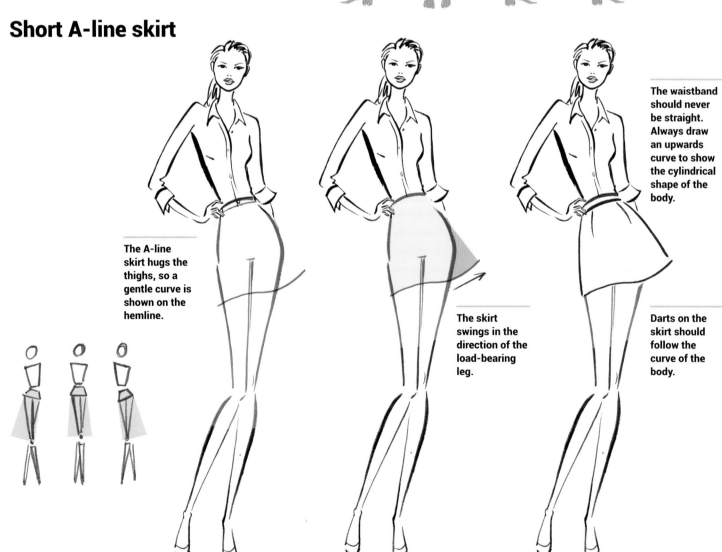

The A-line skirt hugs the thighs, so a gentle curve is shown on the hemline.

The skirt swings in the direction of the load-bearing leg.

The waistband should never be straight. Always draw an upwards curve to show the cylindrical shape of the body.

Darts on the skirt should follow the curve of the body.

Long skirt with pockets

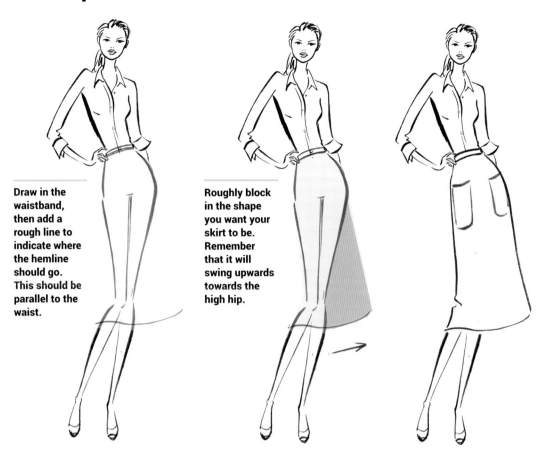

Draw in the waistband, then add a rough line to indicate where the hemline should go. This should be parallel to the waist.

Roughly block in the shape you want your skirt to be. Remember that it will swing upwards towards the high hip.

This skirt falls below the knee, so the fabric will crease at the knee joint. Try to keep features symmetrical by adding a centre front in pencil and keeping pockets parallel to the angle of the waist.

Long gathered skirt

This pose forces the full skirt to swing out to the right.

SHIRTDRESS

Drawing a shirtdress is a great way to discover how the centre front works on top and bottom garments, especially since there is a placket (which is always down the centre front). The design is drawn showing a soft fabric, not a crisp cotton or denim. The folds and fabric create a floaty feel so not much of the figure underneath is visible. With the details of seams, placket, buttons, patch pockets, belt and collar, this can be a demanding subject to draw.

STEP 1

Start by drawing the neckhole and armhole position. Mark the bust and hip angles. The centre line helps you place these markers. Add the waistline and hemline of the skirt, remembering that it will swing to the side of the high hip.

STEP 2

Draw in the basic shape of the shirtdress together with the seam lines (for example, the seam on the bust).

STEP 3

Now add the extra details for the dress, making sure the compression areas and folds give an idea of the type of fabric you wish to represent.

STRIPED DRESSES

These horizontal and vertical striped dresses illustrate how the body, tension and gravity affect the fabric through compression and stretch.

You Will Need
* ★ smooth paper
* ★ HB pencil
* ★ black fine-tipped pen
* ★ marker pens in an assortment of colours

Horizontal stripes

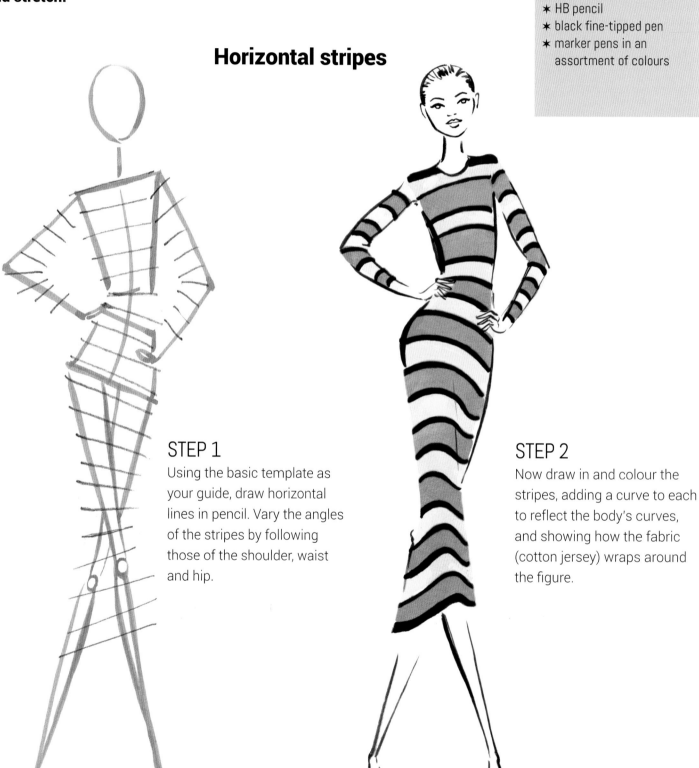

STEP 1

Using the basic template as your guide, draw horizontal lines in pencil. Vary the angles of the stripes by following those of the shoulder, waist and hip.

STEP 2

Now draw in and colour the stripes, adding a curve to each to reflect the body's curves, and showing how the fabric (cotton jersey) wraps around the figure.

Vertical stripes

STEP 1

Here you can see the basic shape of the dress on the template pose of the high-hip walking woman. The skirt of the dress swings in the direction of the high hip. Because the body 'crunches' on the left and stretches on the right, the left profile of the dress will buckle and fold (see orange arrows).

STEP 2

Draw the design of the dress and add the vertical stripes. These will follow the body's curves and the fabric's reaction to the pose, as shown on the left side of the waist.

STEP 3

Add in the colour and show where the stripes expand, following the body's shape and movement.

PATTERNED DRESSES

Colour and pattern make a huge difference to the feel of your images. If you don't know what colours to use, take your inspiration from nature – see how green makes pinks and reds really 'sing'. If in doubt about pattern, use your black linework to hold the image together.

You Will Need

* smooth paper
* HB pencil
* gouache paints in your chosen colours
* black fine-tip marker

Sleeveless

STEP 1
This is a simple, effective way of rendering a two-colour pattern. Draw in the unclothed parts of the figure.

STEP 2
Add the first colourway pattern.

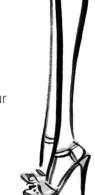

STEP 3
Add the second colour in the white spaces of the fabric. Use a contrasting colour for the shoes.

Tiered

STEP 1
Use this basic template for your busy, patterned dress.

STEP 2
The dress has lots of tiers. The angle of these will alter according to the pose, so map them out first so that you make your figure realistic.

STEP 3
Draw the print of your dress in greater detail in line.

STEP 4
Now paint in the chosen colours using the linework as your guide.

UNDERWEAR AND SWIMWEAR

Look through your references for swimwear or underwear photos. Three-quarter poses are great for showing off the body and are often more interesting than the full frontal pose. The guide shown here is good for any design showing the torso, with the key areas marked.

You Will Need

★ smooth paper
★ HB pencil
★ fine-tip marker pens
  in red and black
★ range of gouache paints
  in your chosen colours

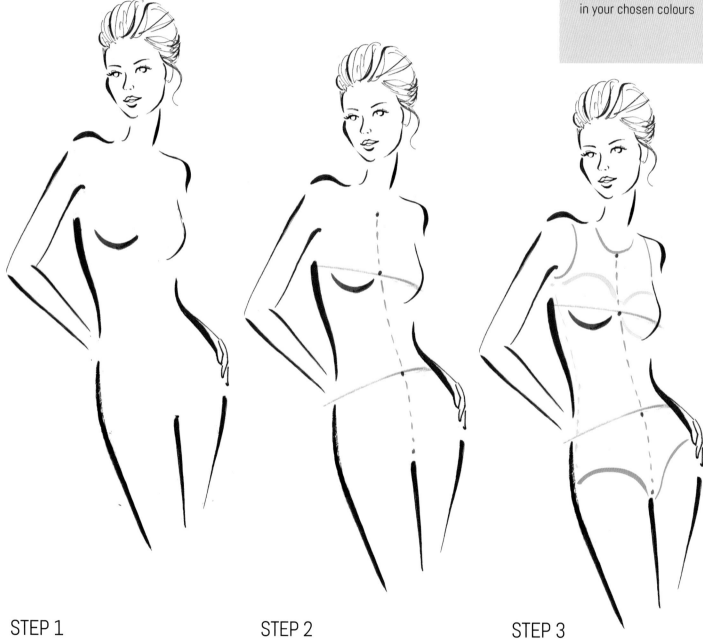

STEP 1
Draw a three-quarter pose, above the knee only. I've chosen an image with a great 'up-do', which will work with a range of garments.

STEP 2
Draw a red dot at the pit of the neck, on the sternum, belly button and crotch. Join up these dots to make your centre line. Add the angles for the breasts and high hip.

STEP 3
Now add the other essential guidelines – neck, shoulder and leg holes. Also add the top of the breast line, as though you are drawing a fitted corset.

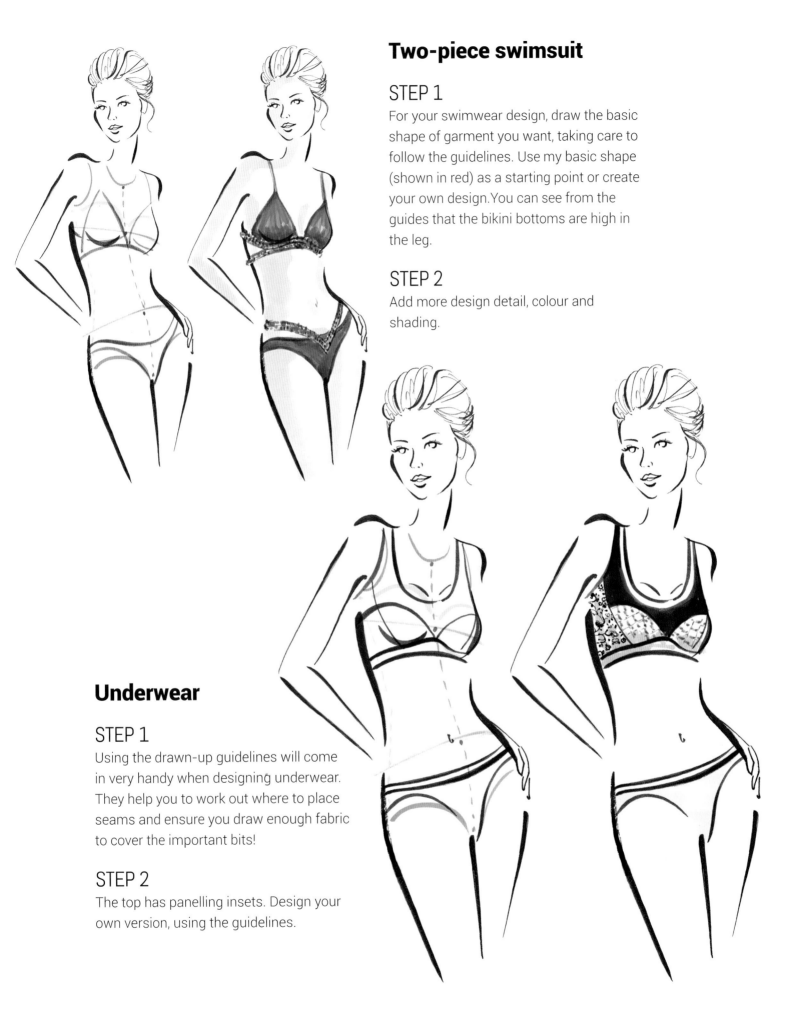

Two-piece swimsuit

STEP 1

For your swimwear design, draw the basic shape of garment you want, taking care to follow the guidelines. Use my basic shape (shown in red) as a starting point or create your own design. You can see from the guides that the bikini bottoms are high in the leg.

STEP 2

Add more design detail, colour and shading.

Underwear

STEP 1

Using the drawn-up guidelines will come in very handy when designing underwear. They help you to work out where to place seams and ensure you draw enough fabric to cover the important bits!

STEP 2

The top has panelling insets. Design your own version, using the guidelines.

CLASSIC MEN'S JACKET

Here we look at designing a sophisticated, classic jacket. If you take it stage by stage, it will be easy. You can also use this guide to design coats; just remember to give the body more room to move and to allow for thicker garments, such as jumpers, beneath.

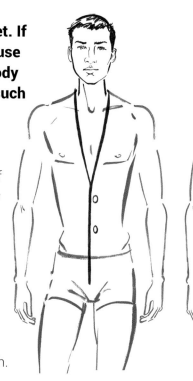
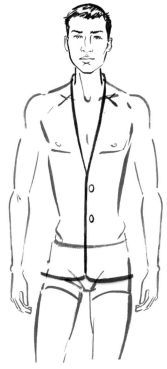

STEP 1

First, find a good torso figure as your guide. On the centre line of your figure, mark where you want the buttons to be. Decide how far down you want the neckline to go – as a rule, most jackets close just below the chest.

STEP 2

Jacket collars are higher than the shoulder line, so make the line of the collar go higher round the back of the neck. Mark the point at which the collar and lapel meet – this is usually around collarbone height. Then mark where you want the jacket to finish.

STEP 3

Now design the lapels. Curve the line of the collar towards the back of the neck. The collar is usually not as wide as the lapel.

STEP 4

Design the overall shape of the jacket. See how the proportions are exaggerated (shown in red). Make sure there is room for the body to move.

STEP 5

Add the rest of the details. How many pockets do you want to show? What angle will they be at? Do you need to show any darts?

Classic jacket – full-length pose

You Will Need
★ smooth watercolour paper
★ HB pencil
★ eraser
★ marker pens in mid-light beige and grey
★ pastel/chalk in a darker colour
★ white chalk or pastel pencil

STEP 1
Here is the jacket with trousers added. The suit is in a soft wool. Add a base colour using a marker pen.

STEP 2
Add some texture to the fabric using a coloured or chalk pencil in a darker shade. Try placing your paper on a rough texture and shading the darker parts of the suit; this will work a bit like a rubbing, letting the texture show through.

STEP 3
Add highlights using a chalk or pastel pencil. Highlight some of the folds, the centre line of the trousers and the lapels. Add some dots of highlight all over for more texture.

STEP 4
Add more depth with a mid-grey marker pen, and colour in the shirt and tie in complementary colours.

DENIM

Drawing denim presents a challenge. A lot of the seams on denim garments are topstitched. The shadows created by this, together with the colour of the stitching, make the seams a major feature of the drawing.

STEP 1
As my starting point, I have taken the catwalk swimwear pose from pages 88-9 and scaled it up using the fashion template measurements.

STEP 2
Draw in the linework. I've drawn the creases in red where the body bends, at the elbow, waist, crotch and knee, and in folds at the bottom of the jeans.

STEP 3
The creases can affect the outline of the garment. Crinkle the silhouette where the folds are drawn; remember that denim is thick, so use rounded bumps (shown in red). Give the figure a wash of light colour for the flesh and the mid-tone of the denims (I'm showing two different denim colours here).

STEP 4
Add shadow to the arms and legs. It should be shaded on the sides of the arms and legs to show the fabric wrapping around the body. This helps to portray a three-dimensional image.

STEP 6

Add extra detail to the figure with more shading, and draw in the buttons.

Draw the topstitch detail on the denim seams – you can use chalk or pastel pencils which will give you fine detail. You will also be able to smudge certain areas to break up the fine detail.

An obvious way to represent the character of denim is to draw the topstitch in orange (the perfect complementary colour for blue). I've used chalk pencils, which give a nice, fine, controlled broken line. You could also paint it on with gouache using a small, fine, pointed brush.

STEP 5

Take some coloured pencils in grey/dark blue and white, and draw in the texture of the denim, trying to keep the lines flowing in the same direction, whether slanted or vertical. Use the darker colours for shadow areas and white for the highlighted areas. Jeans often have highlights (whiskering) on the crotch and knee areas.

TEEN DRESS

Here's how to adapt your pose template for a teenage girl, while also learning to draw flounces and polka dots! Teenagers are lots of fun to draw – full of attitude, tension and self-consciousness and with long, gangly limbs.

The girl in the final picture is aged between 15 and 17, so she has different proportions from the tween on pages 42–3, but they are also different from those of an adult. I want her to have the limb length of adult, but not the same torso bulk or curves. Lots of body angles should help achieve a look that oozes attitude and youthfulness, which is also helped by exaggerated hair, footwear and pattern proportions. The style of dress is baggy, so the body shape is not clearly visible. Her hair is long and a great mauve colour!

You Will Need
★ smooth paper
★ HB pencil
★ eraser
★ black ink and a round brush
★ watercolour paints

Polka-dot dress

STEP 1

The basic template is shown in green. I wanted to create a short, flouncy, tiered, unfitted dress for a teenager. You can see how the angle of the shoulders makes the dress move away from the left side of the body.

STEP 2
I have slimmed the limbs and shrunk the torso to give a more gangly, teen look.

STEP 3
In pencil, mark a grid on the dress for placing the dots.

STEP 4
Draw in the dots that will appear big and less distorted on the garments – these are basically the ones on the flatter areas of the torso.

STEP 5
Now draw in the dots that will appear smaller – on the curved areas at the side of the body and on the frill.

STEP 6
Make sure the dots aren't too evenly spaced out on the frilled tiers, as the frills will create spontaneous distortions. Have fun with the accessories – clashing colours work well.

Draw a flower shape of dots (shown in grey) and just keep repeating it.

The easiest way to draw dots is first to draw a vertical line.

Then draw a dot on one side, halfway between two dots.

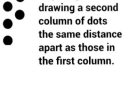

Use this new dot as your guide for drawing a second column of dots the same distance apart as those in the first column.

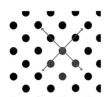

This image shows a diamond pattern of dots.

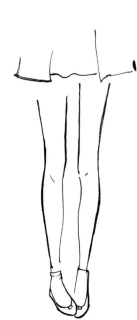

Teens often hold their bodies in awkward poses, which provide the illustrator with a great opportunity to have some fun. A great short cut to suggesting youth is to draw your figure with pigeon toes.

To show the tiers, draw in the seam (black line), then draw two more parallel lines showing the bottom edge of the folded fabric. You'll draw the curved folds between these blue lines.

Draw in the curvy bottom line, then draw the flare lines of the drapery above this. Try to make your drawing look organic and not too symmetrical.

Chapter 6

DRAWING FABRICS

I'm going to show you various ways of rendering fabrics. Each medium has its own qualities that work best for certain fabrics. Watercolours and pastels are great for fur, for example, but fat marker pens are not – although bright fun fur might look good rendered this way. Experiment to see what works for you.

CHECKS AND PINSTRIPES

Here we look at cloth used for coats and suits, such as tweed, plaid, herringbone and houndstooth. The patterns in these woven fabrics usually follow a grid, so pencil this in before you start your design.

HERRINGBONE

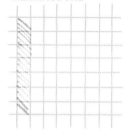

Pencil in a grid to use as a guide. With a fine-tipped marker pen, draw a diagonal line or two in each square.

In the next column draw diagonally in the opposite direction to create a mirror image. Just keep repeating this pattern for a herringbone effect.

HOUNDSTOOTH

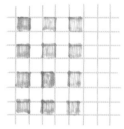

Using a fine-tipped marker pen, colour in alternative squares horizontally and vertically.

Draw a diagonal line in the blank squares in each vertical row.

Do the same in the blank squares in each horizontal row.

CHECKS

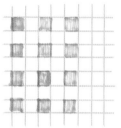

Use the same first stage as for houndstooth.

Fill in the alternative blank horizontal squares with diagonal lines.

On the vertical, draw diagonal lines in between the squares of solid colour only.

Man's checked suit

For this windowpane check suit, rough in the lines in pencil. Curve the horizontal lines downwards where they meet the edge of the figure. The exception to this rule is the right leg, which is receding from view, so the lines go up.

Woman's pinstriped suit

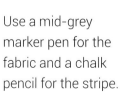

When drawing pinstripes, take time to work out the direction of the stripes. The collars should be angled differently to each other and the jacket front.

Use a mid-grey marker pen for the fabric and a chalk pencil for the stripe.

CHIFFON LACE

Lace with a floral pattern on a fine net base can be beaded for extra embellishment. The fabric is drawn over a skin tone with soft cross-hatching, or you could use the rubbing technique over textured paper.

You Will Need
* smooth watercolour paper
* black fine-tipped pen
* watercolours and round brush

STEP 1
Draw the outline of the figure and garment. In this case, the fabric doesn't have much stretch so add space around the body.

STEP 2
Paint in the parts of the body that will be seen, including any bits that can be seen underneath the chiffon lace.

STEP 3
Now add a wash of colour to all the lace fabric.

STEP 4

Paint the areas of chiffon that aren't covering the limbs, so that they are darker than the flesh colour.

STEP 5

Draw the lace design on the chiffon. Try to draw an interpretation rather than a straight copy.

STEP 6

Add some more shading to the figure. You could scallop the edges of the lace on the neckline and sleeves. You could also show a coloured slip underneath the dress.

I've added a swatch to give you a clearer idea of the lace design, though it's the spirit of the print that's more important than just copying a pattern.

TULLE

The point of this tulle dress is to portray decadence and embellishment. Just remember to draw the fabric more or less to scale on the body (though there's no point drawing to scale if the viewer can't see any of the lovely detail). I've started with a pose taken from a generic catwalk image, although for this style of dress an extreme pose would be great.

STEP 1

Start with the photo reference pose and translate it to your fashion template measurements, drawing very lightly in pencil. Paint in the flesh for the figure in watercolour, not marker pen (this is because the flesh will be seen through the transparent dress). Draw in the detail of the face and dress. Show the pattern of the lace and the construction of the tulle skirt. I haven't drawn in any outline on this image because the skirt has a soft, see-through quality which a hard edge would kill.

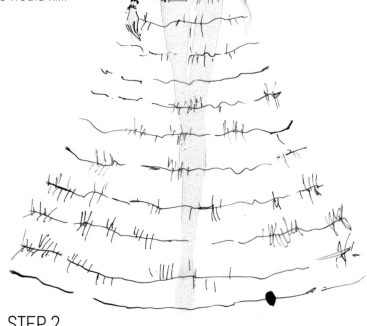

STEP 2

Although the dress is black, don't just fill it in with black as this will not tell the viewer anything about the true quality of the tulle. Either use a dark grey pastel or, as I did here, a powdery eyeshadow drawn on with a sponge applicator then smudged and blended in with the finger. Shade in the basic shape of the dress to show the silhouette. You don't have to add much – just fill in the skirt area. I've also added some shading up the left side of the torso.

STEP 3

Using the same grey, go over and highlight the darker, more concentrated areas of detail to help explain the structure of the dress. The colour should be concentrated in the ruched folds of the tiered tulle trim.

STEP 4

Now concentrate on drawing more detail in a slightly darker shade on the bodice and dress to show the character of the garment.

STEP 5

You need to make the garment more three-dimensional by adding shadow to the darker areas, usually down one side of the figure.

This is the dress rendered in marker pen instead of eyeshadow and watercolour, but still following the same step-by-step guide.

A SIMPLE PLAID

In fashion, plaids can get quite confusing and complex – see, for example, some of Vivienne Westwood's designs. I've kept this plaid quite simple, with a big check and not too many colours.

It will help if you break down the pattern of horizontals and verticals into colours and widths. Scale also plays an important part in the drawing. It isn't always best to represent the check as life-sized in order to get your message across to the viewer. A busy small check will look even busier and messier when reduced to the much smaller scale of your drawing, and something so detailed will probably not be worth the effort. Consider instead trying to capture the essence of the fabric and breaking it down into its most appealing components. As a rule I hold up the swatch to my body or to a toile and see how many times it would repeat widthways; then I reduce it to 25 per cent for my sketch.

You Will Need

* bleedproof paper, smooth
* HB or B pencil
* marker pens – double-ended would be good; if not, chisel-edged in mid-reds and mid-blues
* fine-tip markers in darker blue and red
* I also used ink and pen for the line work and extra marker colours for the head and boots, but these are not essential

STEP 1

First sketch a walking figure, with the weight distributed on the right leg so that the right hip is higher than the left.

These are the angles of the shoulders, waist and hips.

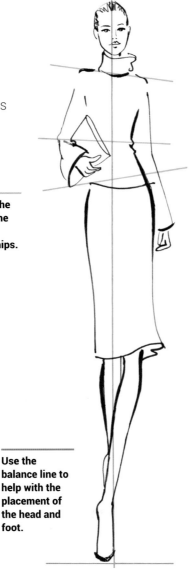

Use the balance line to help with the placement of the head and foot.

STEP 2

Draw in the horizontal stripe on the chest area and distribute the rest of the horizontals on the sweater. There's also a prominent stripe at the bottom of the skirt. You can choose how controlled and detailed you want your own drawing to be – I've kept mine quite loose. Remember, if the garment is tight-fitting the stripes will follow the contours of the body. The skirt has more movement to it than the sweater – the stripes bend around the contours of the body.

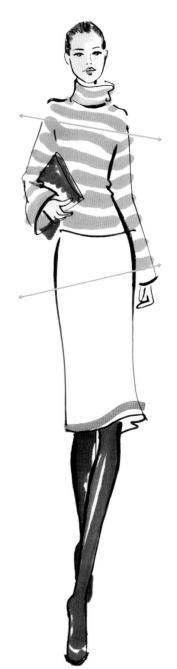

STEP 3

Draw in the vertical lines, making sure they follow the direction of the body. Notice how the top and bottom of the outfit change direction, as shown by the red arrows. This helps to add tension and interest to the image.

Direction of body changes at the waist.

STEP 4

Add secondary vertical and horizontal stripes, maybe in a different colour. Draw some texture to help show the weave.

STEP 5

Go over the horizontal and vertical stripes with marker pen to darken where they intersect. I haven't painted them all in. I feel it's better to leave some free so that the image feels a bit looser and doesn't start to resemble a scanned fabric, but it's up to you to choose the effect you want. Finally, add a shadow to the whole left side to give your drawing more depth.

A BOLD PRINT

This a fun way with colouring, great for those who like a more 'craft' approach to illustration. Here you cut the figure out of card and place it over a custom-made fabric print. Before computers, this was a technique I employed a lot. I even used it to produce a series of 1.2m (4ft) fashion sketches for the windows at Liberty in London.

In Photoshop you can achieve this result by creating layered images – first scanning in your drawing and filling it with solid colour, then deleting the colour and using this opaque layer and adding a print layer underneath.

You Will Need

* smooth paper
* HB pencil
* card
* black marker pen
* strong colours in the medium of your choice – gouache, ink or coloured paper
* scalpel
* cutting board
* glue stick

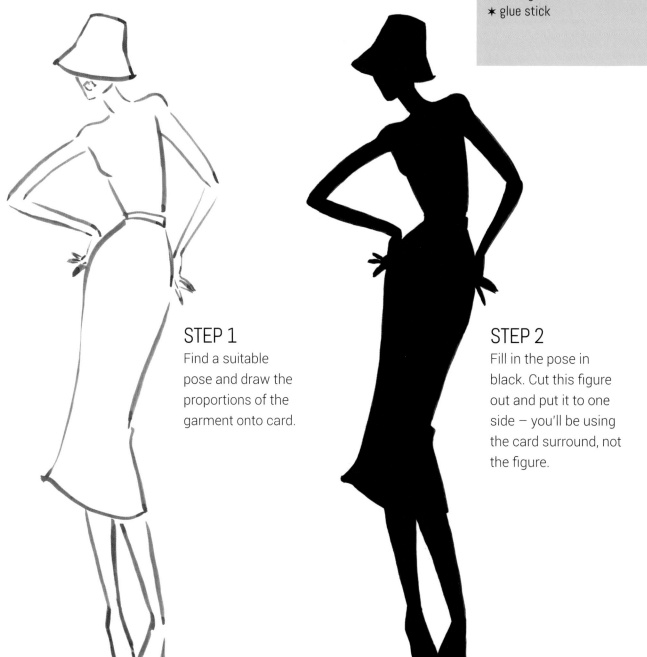

STEP 1
Find a suitable pose and draw the proportions of the garment onto card.

STEP 2
Fill in the pose in black. Cut this figure out and put it to one side – you'll be using the card surround, not the figure.

STEP 3

This is a graphic, bold, simple colour print. You can use gouache, ink or collage to render it on paper.

STEP 4

Place the card from which you have cut out the figure over the painted print. Move it around to find the most effective use of the pattern.

STEP 5

By leaving out detail and letting the print fill the whole image, your finished version can look quite abstract. Alternatively, use flesh-coloured paper and cut out the detail of the face and hands (I've already added lips to the face and shading to these elements to anchor the image).

A FLORAL PRINT

This lovely, heavy linen summer dress has a strong silhouette with a deep, plunging neckline. When drawing patterns try to get a swatch of fabric to use as reference. Work out roughly how many times the print will go across the body then transfer this to your drawing.

STEP 1

Start with this 50s summer dress – the skirt hugs the hips, then the silhouette changes as it billows out.

STEP 2

Add the base colour – I've rendered it in watercolour. The brushstrokes follow the movement of the skirt, radiating out from the waist. The colour also undulates; this is achieved by the application of paint to wet watercolour paper with a wet brush.

STEP 3

Use a chalk pencil to start the bold flower print.

STEP 4

I used Photoshop here. I added an extra layer to the scanned image and applied the pink flower detail to this. I was then able to adjust the colours.

STEP 5

This is the finished version with the Photoshopped pink and green flower layer made transparent to show the blue colour.

SEQUINS

This sexy, hip-hugging, sequinned evening dress has a fishtail skirt and cutout detail.

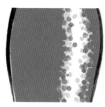

A close-up showing how to render sequins and shine.

You Will Need

* watercolour paper
* black ink and a brush cartridge pen
* 3 or 4 marker pens in shades of one colour
* white chalk pencil or gouache
* watercolours for the figure details

Sequin dress

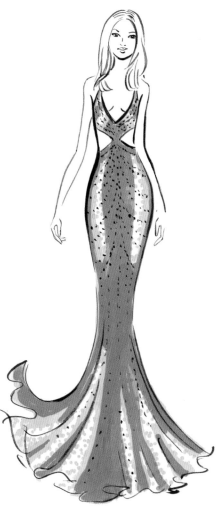

STEP 1

Draw the design using the brush cartridge pen. Use the palest shade of marker pen all over the garment, but leave the lightest, most reflective parts of the dress white.

STEP 2

With the marker pen, soften the line between the white spaces and the soft colour, using small dots. Don't fill the whole white space with dots, just use them at the edges.

STEP 3

With a mid-tone marker pen, colour the second shade, leaving some space so that the first layer and the highlights show.

STEP 4
Again with the mid-tone marker pen, add little dots to the lighter shade, leaving gaps.

STEP 5
With an even darker pen, repeat step 3 for your final layer.

STEP 6
Repeat the same process as for step 4, not covering up too much and making sure that the lovely layers show through.

STEP 7
Now it's time to add sparkle. For this, use chalk pencil or white gouache on top of the layers. Only concentrate on a few areas for this – down one side, with a few sparkles added to the darkest area.

STEP 8
Finish off the figure in watercolours and pick out details on the dress in black ink.

SATIN

There is a lot to consider when rendering satin – the shine, the figure underneath the fabric, and the folds. Shine is likely to occur at tension points such as the bust, hips and forward thigh/knee.

You Will Need

* smooth paper
* black fine-tipped pen
* gouache or marker pen in mid-blue
* pastel in a lighter and a darker blue
* watercolour paints for the figure details

Make sure you draw the right folds for the fabric – silk and satin both fall heavily in big folds from the torso to the floor. They also have smaller angular folds around the body at stress points, for example, at the shoulder and waist.

This bias-cut dress clings to the hips, falls away at the knees, and ends in a pool of fabric on the floor.

Satin can flow around the body to great effect, especially on a bias-cut evening gown.

Here I've demonstrated how the light bounces off a tubular object; this is a version of how the light will react on the fabric.

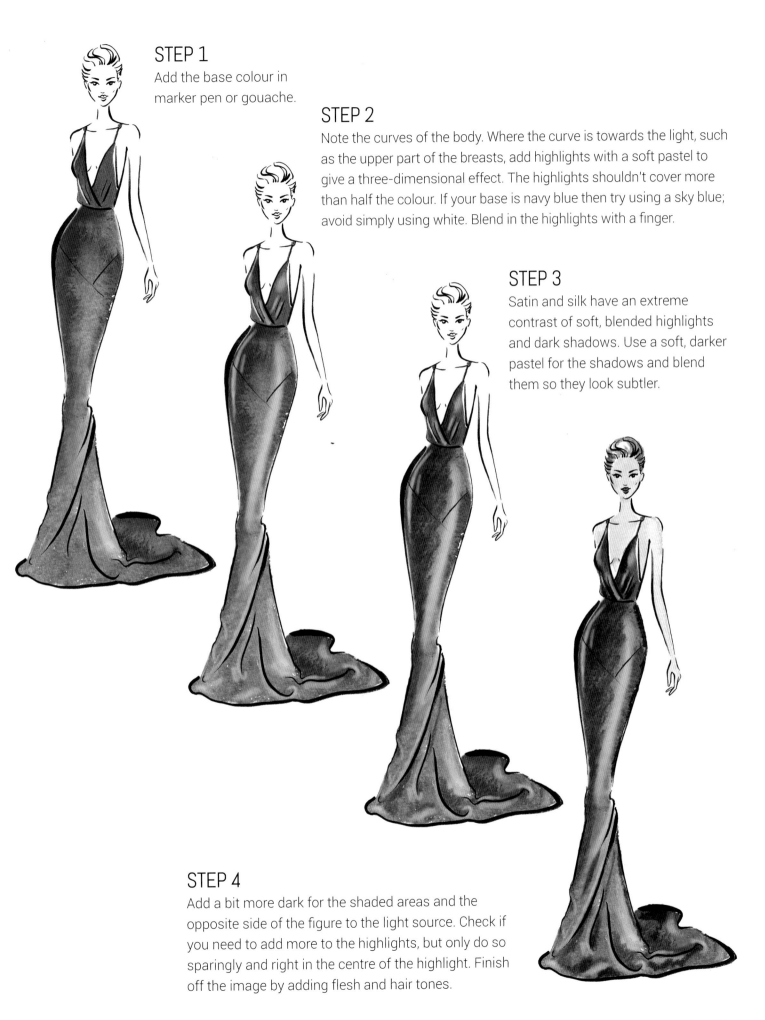

STEP 1
Add the base colour in marker pen or gouache.

STEP 2
Note the curves of the body. Where the curve is towards the light, such as the upper part of the breasts, add highlights with a soft pastel to give a three-dimensional effect. The highlights shouldn't cover more than half the colour. If your base is navy blue then try using a sky blue; avoid simply using white. Blend in the highlights with a finger.

STEP 3
Satin and silk have an extreme contrast of soft, blended highlights and dark shadows. Use a soft, darker pastel for the shadows and blend them so they look subtler.

STEP 4
Add a bit more dark for the shaded areas and the opposite side of the figure to the light source. Check if you need to add more to the highlights, but only do so sparingly and right in the centre of the highlight. Finish off the image by adding flesh and hair tones.

TAFFETA

Taffeta is a great fabric for creating volume without bulk. It will stand away from the body and has plenty of shine, as you can see from the folds of this ballgown.

STEP 1

This is a dramatic taffeta dress with a very full skirt. Taffeta has a crisp, starchy quality and the fabric will stand away from the body in sharp, broken lines. The belt is great for reining in the fabric and showing some of the figure underneath to create a more flattering silhouette. I used ink on a dry brush, but pen and ink would also be good for this figure.

STEP 2

Use marker pen or gouache to colour in the lightest shade. Taffeta is very reflective, so leave lots of areas white to show the shine. Try to have these areas near fold lines and where the fabric buckles.

STEP 3

Add a darker shade in marker pen to show the really shaded areas in the creases. Cover about half the lighter colour. Taffeta has strong colour changes – you want it to go from fold/dark to mid-tone to shine, and then back to fold/dark.

STEP 4

Taffeta is sometimes shot with a different colour, which only shows up in the shine. It is usually a contrasting colour (red taffeta is often shot with green, khaki with pink, and so on). This adds to the drama of the fabric when it's in motion and makes a striking illustration. This blue/purple fabric is shot with pink, so use pink marker pen on some of the bigger white areas, but don't add more than a line or two.

A red/green version of the same illustration.

A khaki/pink version.

NET

Tulle and net have a lovely transparent quality, but they are quite crisp and stand away from the body in a starchy manner. They are great for romantic evening dresses, for a big statement silhouette.

STEP 1

Draw the figure and the outline of the net dress. The pose is very simple. Paint in the background with mid-grey ink or marker pen, being careful not to go over the silhouette.

STEP 2

Redraw the dress using pastel, smudging the linework to create an ethereal look.

You Will Need

* smooth paper
* HB pencil
* mid-grey marker pen or ink for the background
* fine-tipped black pen
* pastels in shades of white, beige and light grey
* coloured chalk pencils or pastels for embellishment

STEP 3

Now get bolder with the pastels so that the dress becomes more opaque. Try to leave some areas less worked to give the impression of lots of translucent layers. There is more build-up of colour where the fabric gathers near the waist, as there would be on the real garment.

STEP 4

Use pastels for the face and arms, keeping the look soft and feminine. Add the embroidery details using sharpened chalk pencils or coloured pastels.

KNITWEAR

Knitwear stretches and gives around the body, so it's not necessary to draw darts and fewer seams are needed. Garments vary from tight, figure-hugging sweaters to loose, oversized, bulky knits that swamp the figure.

When designing knitwear, once you have drawn the basic shape, draw in the direction lines of the different stitches as a guide. Either use pencil, which you can rub out later, or trace over on a separate sheet of paper.

Examine and draw different types of knit to gain a greater understanding of how the stitches work.

Chalk pencils are also good for knitwear, giving a soft, blurred line, similar to a strand of wool.

Ribbed and rolled edges can add extra emphasis to sleeves and necklines. Use your guide to help draw the correct flowing knit. Don't fill in all the garment with stitches, but leave areas free to keep the sketch looking fresh.

Here pen and ink is used to great effect for a spidery knit.

Crochet dress

STEP 1

This is an edgy design, with lots of intricate details. Start with a line version as your guide. Using pen and ink for crochet creates a lovely spidery feel.

You Will Need

★ watercolour paper
★ B1 pencil
★ dipping nibs in various sizes (try mapping or sketching nibs)
★ black ink, preferably waterproof
★ watercolour paints
★ round brush, no. 6–12

STEP 2

Next add the flesh tone to the figure and to any areas that might show through the fabric.

STEP 3

Put in the heavy, dark details using a dry brush and black ink.

STEP 4

Add more colour, still using the dry brush technique. This type of fabric needs a wispy, delicate touch – nothing too solid or heavy. The blue helps to anchor the figure.

STEP 5

Finally add the complementary orange colour for the extra detail, highlighting some of the stitching.

LEATHER

Here you can see how to render leather in a classic jean cut, tight at the hip and thigh and a little looser on the lower leg. Leather is a perennial favourite in runway shows, synonymous with a sexy, rock-chick attitude and the quest for cool. The same rules for creases and shine can be applied to drawing leather boots.

You Will Need
★ smooth paper
★ fine-tipped black marker pen or black ink and a round brush, no. 6–12
★ white/light grey pastel or chalk pencil

STEP 1

Pick a pose that will show all the design elements of these leather jeans. Classic leather jeans are very tight, especially on the thigh. They become a bit looser towards the bottom of the leg. Work out the waistband length and width and the belt loops.

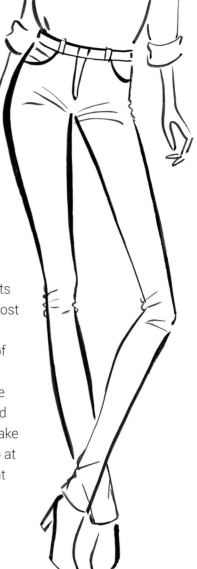

STEP 2

Tight leather trousers have lots of small folds and creases, most of which are horizontal, apart from those in the lower part of the leg. Creases tend to be at the crotch, radiating out to the side of the hip, at the knee and at the bottom of the jeans. Make sure the waistband curves up at the ends and isn't just straight across.

STEP 3
Start adding the colour to the leather. I've marked the area you need to leave free of colour in red. These are the highlights on the folds and down either side of the leg. They will vary in thickness, so don't be too precise.

STEP 4
Paint in the dark area. There should be a sharp contrast between the two areas, with no softness. Use brush and ink or, as in this case, marker pen. If you fill in too much colour, wait until it's dry and add some white gouache

STEP 5
Now add even more shine to the leather, using pastel or chalk pencil down the centre of each leg. You can smudge and add more white/light grey if you like.

VELVET

This classic red velvet smoking suit has wide trousers and a buttoned waistcoat. If you don't have these red marker colours, use marker pens in two different shades of any colour of your choice. For a subtle look, try layering the colours before they dry so that they smudge and bleed into each other.

You Will Need
★ smooth paper
★ round brush, no. 6–12
★ black ink
★ marker pens in 2 or 3 shades of the same colour
★ flesh-tone marker pen

STEP 1
I used a Chinese brush to draw this velvet suit in a high-hip pose.

STEP 2
Use marker pen to shade in the base colour, leaving a margin for shine at the edges of the garment (near the linework). Velvet has a big step in colour on the shine, so be aware of the direction the light is coming from (in this case, the right).

STEP 3
Take a lighter shade of marker pen and colour in the highlighted areas, blending in.

STEP 4
After I finished the image, I felt that the waist needed to be darkened more and shadow needed adding elsewhere to give more tone. I added a darker shade on the areas that were facing away from the light source.

TWEED

This is quite a complicated way of rendering tweed, but it's very effective. You can either render the suit in bold contrasting colours, as here, or in more natural, earthy shades.

STEP 1

Start with a basic high-hip walking pose, taking account of the angles of shoulder and hip.

STEP 2

Draw in the basic shape of your garment. The blue areas show the space around the figure and the direction in which the skirt swings.

You Will Need

★ heavy smooth paper or card
★ HB or B pencil
★ eraser
★ tissue paper in 2 colours
★ glue stick or PVA
★ ruler
★ scalpel
★ watercolour paints
★ white chalk pencil or gouache

STEP 3

Add more detail to the suit design and draw a rough grid as reference for your tweed pattern.

STEP 4

Cut strips of tissue paper in the colours you need. I've used blue and red. Work out which colour needs to be stuck down first in order to achieve the right effect. I started by using vertical blue stripes, leaving a corresponding white space between them.

STEP 5

Stick down horizontal blue stripes, leaving a gap double their width between them. Make the stripes parallel to the shoulder angle on the jacket and to the hip angle on the skirt.

STEP 6

Fill in the horizontal gaps between the blue stripes with two stripes of red. Try not to let the stripe go over the linework – use a scalpel blade to make a clean cut.

STEP 7

The tweed is getting busy, so take care as you place a vertical red stripe between the blue vertical stripes.

STEP 8

The all important finishing touches: on each square of colour draw a little + at each corner with a chalk pencil or white gouache. Paint in the figure's features with watercolour. Saturate the boots and blouse with water and let strong watercolours bleed into these areas.

FAUX FUR

I'm going to show you two ways of drawing faux fur: first, with pastel or powdered eye makeup; secondly, with watercolour or gouache.

You Will Need
* ★ smooth paper
* ★ H1 pencil
* ★ fine-tipped black marker pen
* ★ light and mid-tone pink pastels
* ★ grey, black and white pastels
* ★ darker chalk pencil in pink or purple
* ★ tissue for smudging/blending
* ★ round brush, no. 6–12
* ★ finer brush for facial details
* ★ watercolour in carmine red
* ★ watercolours for hair and facial features
* ★ charcoal pencil

STEP 1
Draw your figure and lightly draw in the garment – bear in mind that fur is voluminous and will add extra bulk to the body.

STEP 2
Take a soft pastel in a mid-tone colour and shade the coat all over (not too light and not too dark).

STEP 3
Using your finger, smudge the colours in the direction of the fur. The colour shouldn't be even, but should have shades of light and dark to reflect the model's pose. Pick out areas you think should be darker (for more depth) and shade in a slightly darker colour, making your marks different shapes and sizes. Smudge these new marks. Now pick an even darker shade (maybe grey or black if the base colour isn't too light) and add fine, sparse marks in delicate strokes. You can add some marks to the side of the garment, slightly smudging them in the direction of the fur.

STEP 4
Erase the pencil lines. Add a highlight in white or a pale version of the base colour. These highlights will help to show the character and length of the fur. As a final touch, use a fine coloured pencil in a darker shade to emphasize the furriness. Remember to use sparingly – you can always add more later.

STEP 1
Draw the line
of your figure
in pencil.

STEP 2
Wet the paper – the
blue line shows the
area you need to wet –
then add colour with a
very wet colour-loaded
brush.

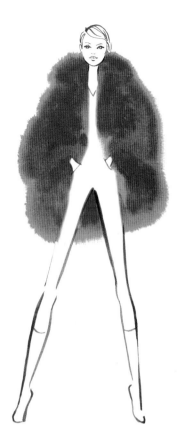

STEP 3
Wait for the paper to dry, then
add the linework and the other
element of the image, apart
from the coat.

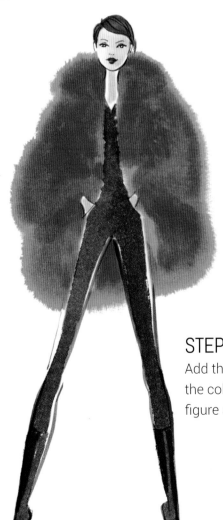

STEP 4
Add the rest of
the colour to the
figure and face.

STEP 5
With black marker pen, add detail
to the coat with short strokes
to represent the fur. Use broken
lines to indicate collar and
sleeves. Use a charcoal pencil
for soft, smudged lines. If you
don't like the marks, just smudge
them away and start again.

ANIMAL PRINTS

You can have lots of fun drawing animal prints, from ultra-realistic to highly stylized. It's not necessary to use natural colours – try mauves and blues for maximum impact.

Use a pale colour for the base.

Draw some random oval shapes – they don't have to be precise and the edges can be rough.

Surround the oval shapes with 'M' and 'U' marks. You can use random combinations and vary the thicknesses.

You Will Need

★ smooth paper
★ HB pencil
★ eraser
★ marker pens in 4 shades, for example, soft beige, light brown, dark brown and black
★ black ink and a brush or fine-tipped pen

Leopard print dress

STEP 1
Draw your basic high-hip pose and dress outline.

STEP 2
Use a pale shade for the base colour. Add a darker shade in coloured pencil down the middle – it should be quite subtle.

STEP 3
Add blobs of the print in varying sizes, randomly, in a colour that shows up against the background.

STEP 4
Draw around the blob shapes in a darker colour (black or dark brown). Surround them in 'M' and 'U' marks.

Zebra print dress

Draw a wavy line of fluctuating width.

Add another line flowing next to the first. Try not to copy the first line exactly.

Add a line on the other side; this time, split it in two at the end.

Add some extra lines of various widths and some lines where the line is broken or forms a 'V'.

Continue to make lines of various thicknesses, using all the different types of line in a random manner.

STEP 1
Here is a flowing summer frock, perfect for adding an animal print design.

STEP 2
The lines can flow in any direction, whatever works best for your design. You can also vary the scale – smaller for the bodice, larger for the skirt, for example.

PICTURE CREDITS
Page 9, top: Corbis (1918/Christie's Images)
Page 9, bottom: Corbis (Condé Nast Archive)

With thanks to 'big sis' Lynda for checking
my grammar, Mum and Norman for
patience and cups of tea and Andrew for
his sharp tongue and clear vision.

TREND WATCHING
www.WGSN.com
www.pinterest.com
www.whatiwore drawings.blogspot.co.uk
www.vogue.com
www.dazeddigital.com
www.elle.com
i-d.vice.com
www.lofficielmode.com
www.oystermag.com
thepop.com
thelovemagazine.co.uk
www.visionaireworld.com